LECTURE NOTES ON PSYCHIATRY

A

LECTURE NOTES ON
PSYCHIATRY

JAMES WILLIS
MB, FRCP(Edin), MRCPsych, DPM

Consultant Psychiatrist
Guy's Hospital, London
Kings College Hospital, London and
Bexley Hospital, Kent

FOURTH EDITION

BLACKWELL SCIENTIFIC PUBLICATIONS
OXFORD LONDON EDINBURGH MELBOURNE

ISBN 0 632 00571 8

FIRST PUBLISHED 1964
REPRINTED 1966
SECOND EDITION 1968
REPRINTED 1970
THIRD EDITION 1972
FOURTH EDITION 1974

Distributed in the United States of America by
J. B. Lippincott Company, Philadelphia
and in Canada by
J. B. Lippincott Company of Canada Ltd, Toronto

Printed in Great Britain by
Western Printing Services Ltd, Bristol
and bound at Kemp Hall Bindery,
Osney Mead, Oxford

CONTENTS

Acknowledgements   vii

An Introduction to Psychiatry   ix

1   The History—Some Terms Defined—
The Examination   1

2   Affective Disorders   17

3   Schizophrenia   39

4   Organic Syndromes   53

5   Abnormal Personality, Psychopathy
and Hysteria   66

6   Obsessional Illness   75

7   Alcoholism and Drug Dependence   79

8   Subnormality   89

9   Psychiatric Disorders in the Elderly   100

10   Psychiatry and the Law   106

11   Treatment   111

Index   129

ACKNOWLEDGEMENTS

ACKNOWLEDGEMENTS TO 1ST EDITION

This book could not have been written without the encouragement of many former teachers and colleagues. Dr David Stafford-Clark was chief among these. Dr Colin McEvedy gave much valuable advice and Miss D. Harlow typed the manuscripts. The publishers, Mr Per Saugman particularly, have been extremely patient throughout and for this I am most grateful.

ACKNOWLEDGEMENTS TO 2ND EDITION

I should like to express my gratitude to Professor Jack Tizard and Dr Ronald MacKeith for their advice on the re-written chapter on Subnormality. Also Dr Stephen MacKeith for his perceptive comments and helpful criticism.

AN INTRODUCTION TO PSYCHIATRY

Medical students often say that they find psychiatry interesting but disappointing. Interesting because psychiatry is a clinical subject and all students seem to like this, disappointing because as they frequently put it 'it all seems vague and woolly', also they are put off by the apparent lack of a sound body of psychiatric knowledge and the disagreements about diagnosis and treatment.

This book is not intended as a comprehensive text, the length and omissions should make that clear. It is written to try and answer the sort of questions that students seem to need answering fairly quickly when they start a psychiatric clerkship. They find themselves in difficulties because they have to learn a new language and acquire a new set of concepts of illness if they are to retain any interest in psychiatry at all. Too often they are discouraged from trying and emerge as doctors with blind spots for psychological illness.

The training of Medical students remains a subject for discussion, research and revision but as yet it does not adequately prepare the majority of students for much more than a somewhat unwary first encounter with the practice of psychiatry. Students tend to have heard that psychiatry is a discipline 'by schisms rent asunder' and this may make them unnecessarily sceptical, particularly if their half notions are reinforced by the misinformation still so freely available from an intriguing range of sources.

Also there *are* unresolved dilemmas about what things should be taught. Certain medical schools may favour a clinical approach based on traditional diagnosis, treatment and prognosis. Others favour early introduction of the student to psychological principles—showing him how human behaviour may be governed by unconscious processes and relating this to interpersonal relationships and *their* consequences in people's life styles and behaviour. Whilst others have suggested that students need to be introduced quite early to the practice of psychotherapy—since this will provide them with a living illustration of human psychopathology. But while these divisions of opinions may exist (since as yet no one has *proved* what are the needs of students), at least we see the beginnings of a medical student training in which the importance is stressed of the patient as an individual and as a social being—not a mere collection of mechanical systems.

Medical student training may be the subject of discussion, research and revision, but the fact is that it does not equip students for the easy assimilation of psychiatric attitudes and ideas.

For a start the student finds that he needs to re-examine his own concept of disease. Up to now he has had no difficulty in seeing that patients with tumours, fractures, diabetes etc., are in diseased states. His psychiatric patient, on the other hand, often appears well and disclaims symptoms; no handicap is obvious until he finds that the patient's inner life is dominated by a series of fantastic beliefs which have caused him to alter his way of living so that he is now in hospital—maybe against his will. What does he make of that? Is he ill? Are there many patients like that and if so what is wrong with them?

Psychiatry deals with this sort of patient and many others; what they all have in common is disturbances affecting their behaviour, emotions, thinking and perception. Perhaps most important of all is the recognition that 'psychiatric illness' occurs when these disturbances are real changes which persist and exceed commonly accepted limits of normality and are changes about which the patient may complain, be bothered and puzzled about—so that we are justified in regarding them as symptoms. This is the psychiatric frame of reference. We can set it down more formally by saying that we recognize psychiatric illness by examining the patient's

(1) behaviour,
(2) mood,
(3) perception,
(4) thought content,
(5) intelligence level,
(6) memory,   } cognitive
(7) concentration,   functions
(8) orientation in space and time,

and by discerning abnormalities make a clinical diagnosis.

The manifestations of psychiatric disorder can be recognized without great difficulty. The medical student's difficulty in examining psychiatric patients can be traced to:

(1) lack of method,
(2) lack of practice.

It is our intention in this work to provide a simple clinical guide to psychiatric language and syndromes.

The student should always remember:

(1) to listen carefully,
(2) to record conscientiously,
(3) to avoid interpreting and speculating about what he supposes the patient means,
(4) to get a history from as many informants as possible,
(5) only to use words that he understands.

CLASSIFICATION OF MENTAL ILLNESS

The ideal classification would be based on aetiology. In psychiatry this is rarely possible except in certain organic disorders (e.g. G.P.I., delirium tremens), so that classification tends to be descriptive, that is to say based on the dominant observable features of the syndrome (e.g. anxiety, depression). This is unsatisfactory but inevitable at present. The danger of the descriptive method lies in the possibility that the name given to a syndrome may assign to it a separate existence. For example we may talk about schizophrenia without assuming that there is a 'thing' schizophrenia. If the word is allowed to assume a concrete reality this stifles further enquiry.

Classification then may be unsatisfactory but necessary since we have to achieve some sort of order. Many systems are used, some are more satisfactory than others. In this work we will use this classification: it is clinical, oversimple no doubt, but adequate.

Schizophrenia	Simple
	Hebephrenic
	Catatonic
	Paranoid
Affective disorders	Anxiety
	Depression
	Mania and hypomania
Organic states	Delirium and subacute delirium
	Dementia
Hysteria	Hysterical personality
	Conversion hysteria
Personality disorder	Abnormal personalities
	Psychopathy
Obsessional disorder	
Subnormality	
Severe subnormality	

CHAPTER 1. THE HISTORY—
SOME TERMS DEFINED—
THE EXAMINATION

The psychiatric history, like any other, is an attempt to set down an accurate account of an illness. It is taken in the usual way but the technique should be modified to permit the patient to tell his story without becoming unnecessarily distressed. Distress and misery are commonplace since so often the history refers to painful topics. The patient should be allowed to start off wherever he likes in the history rather than adhering to a rigid scheme of questioning—there should be time to sort out all the data afterwards.

THE FIRST INTERVIEW

One should attempt to take as full a history as possible on this occasion but it may not be a practical nor a humane possibility. This first interview is likely to be an event of great significance for the patient—he may have been dreading it or preparing himself for it for days and when it is over it is something he is likely to remember. With this in mind the doctor should do all he can to make the experience bearable for the patient and resist the temptation to question like a cross-examining attorney.

(a) How to elicit a history
Students often complain that they don't know what questions to ask the patient and are surprised when a more skilled examiner unearths facts they had missed. The answer to this difficulty is relatively simple. A history, after all, is only an

edited series of answers to an elaborate and unstructured questionnaire and with practice the expert learns what questions to ask, and constructs his own questionnaire. Listening to others taking a history illustrates this very well—actually this is as good a way of learning to take a history as any, and not widely enough used.

(b) Symptoms and signs

Modes of presentation and symptomatology are of a different order in psychiatry, though not inevitably so. One patient complains of bodily symptoms, another brings a story of persecution by others, whilst another complains of altered mood and poor concentration. Many patients have no complaint at all and deny all symptoms, the history being given by relatives who tell a different story.

(c) The relationship

The relationship between doctor and patient starts as the patient comes through the door. The patient's initial greeting may be friendly, hostile, suspicious or just neutral. Whatever it is the doctor stands to lose or gain a great deal by his own behaviour. There is no substitute for *friendly politeness* and no place for patronizing pseudo-omniscience. The patient should be accepted as he is and not subjected to value judgements. The talkative patient should be permitted to tell his story as he likes at first, and then be guided through the areas that the doctor wants to cover so that a comprehensive history can be taken. The reticent patient needs encouragement, and although this can be difficult, one must not put words in the patient's mouth.

THE PLACE OF HISTORY TAKING IN DIAGNOSIS

There is a fashionable tendency for some psychiatrists to decry diagnosis, to question the 'medical model' of psychiatric illness. And there is good sense in many such criticisms. Just because a person consults a psychiatrist this does not automatically confer on him the status of being ill. This needs to be mentioned for some psychiatrists talk as if they believed that this were the case! Practical psychiatry should remain a clinical subject in which traditional medical training in diagnosis etc. are of clear usefulness without being overvalued. The clinical approach remains to date a humane and pragmatic one. We should recognize too that the clinician has always to be aware of how it is individual and psychological and social forces may influence the content of an illness but not the form of clinical syndromes—and form is what diagnosis is about. Perhaps we would do well always to remember the large gaps in our knowledge and resist the temptation to conceal them with all embracing theories which illuminate all and clarify nothing save their continued existence as untested and untestable hypotheses—ugly white elephants which retain our mistakes long after we have forgotten them.

Diagnosis is made by examination of the mental state. The history contributes to our understanding of the mental state—it is a pointer to the diagnosis. History taking takes time. One cannot learn much about a patient in five minutes or even fifty, for that matter. There is no place in good psychiatry or good medical practice for the 'spot diagnosis'—in psychiatry it generally turns out to be no diagnosis at all. Most diagnostic errors can be traced to poor history taking.

A scheme for history taking
A formal scheme has to be used for writing down the history. This does not mean that one has to take it down in the following order.

COMPLAINT
This should consist merely of a short statement of the patient's complaint, or if he has none, a short statement of the reason for his referral for psychiatric opinion.

FAMILY HISTORY

In this one should enumerate the *parents* and *siblings*, noting carefully such details as *ages, employment, illnesses, causes of death*. It should also include where possible some account of the incidence of any *familial psychiatric illnesses*. Direct questions should always be asked about incidence in the family of epilepsy, delinquency, alcoholism and drug use, suicide and attempted suicide. The family history too should give some information about the *social status* and *inter personal relationships* within the family.

PERSONAL HISTORY

This should commence with a note of the date and place of birth. Any information available about the patient's infant development should be recorded with particular reference to *health* during childhood, *neurotic symptoms* and *infant milestones*. *School record* should next be noted down, concentrating not only on the names of the schools and the leaving age etc., but attempting if possible to state the individual's attainments at school and estimate his social popularity etc. *Occupations* should next be considered in chronological order with wages earned and status. These details may throw some light on the person's pre-morbid personality and also on the evolution of the illness since frequently work performance is impaired by psychiatric illness—it may even be the presenting complaint e.g. 'can't seem to cope with my job—keep having to change my job—can't settle to anything'. It is also useful to make some note of the individual's relationships with employers and colleagues.

MENSTRUAL AND PSYCHO-SEXUAL HISTORY

This includes the usual menstrual history with the addition of psycho-sexual topics such as how the patient acquired sexual information, his/her *varieties* and *frequency of sexual practice* and *fantasy*. The marital history should be noted with details of *engagement, marriage* and *pregnancies* and their outcome.

There should always be careful enquiry about psychiatric disturbance during and after pregnancy.

PAST ILLNESSES
Recorded chronologically.   With details of any admissions and treatments received.

PAST PSYCHIATRIC ILLNESSES
Recorded chronologically.

PRE-MORBID PERSONALITY
An attempt should be made to describe as accurately as possible the individual's personality before the illness. This is the part of the history that usually causes the great difficulty since our methods of describing the personality are so imperfect. In practice, the most helpful descriptions of the pre-morbid personality are not those which consist merely of one or two adjectives but rather those which give a portrait of the individual, consisting of a few paragraphs.

DESCRIPTION OF PRESENT ILLNESS
This should be a detailed chronological account of the illness from the onset to the present time. There should always be an accurate description of the order, mode and speed of the change in the person's symptomatology.

THE PSYCHIATRIC EXAMINATION

The examination of the patient does not stop short at the examination of his mental state but includes a general physical examination, and where needed, physical investigation. Many individuals referred to a psychiatrist turn out to have either associated physical disease or else disease causing their altered mental state. Examples of the latter would be such conditions as cerebral tumours, general paresis, disseminated sclerosis and

B

myxoedema. The physical examination, too, has a positive value in the reassurance of a hypochondriacal patient.

PSYCHIATRIC LANGUAGE—A FEW TERMS DEFINED

Before going any further into details of how we examine and describe the mental state, here is a list of commonly used psychiatric terms.

Anxiety
A feeling of fear or apprehension commonly accompanied by autonomic disturbance. Anxiety may be felt by healthy subjects in the face of stress such as examinations etc., but is described as morbid anxiety when it pervades the mental life of an individual.

Depression
Pathological mood disturbance resembling sadness or grief. Depression is described as reactive when it can be related to an apparent causal agent, and endogenous when it appears out of the blue. The mood change is accompanied by characteristic disturbance of sleep, energy and thinking.

Dementia
Progressive, irreversible intellectual impairment. Dementia is caused by organic brain disease.

Delirium
An organic mental state in which altered consciousness is combined with psychomotor overactivity, hallucinosis and disorientation.

Depersonalization
A subjective feeling of altered reality of the self, e.g. 'I'm not

myself any more. I feel as if I were dead; I feel unreal. Different to what I was. If only I could wake up.'

Derealization
A subjective feeling of altered reality of the environment, e.g. 'Everything around me seems strange like in a dream. Things don't look or feel the same,' usually associated with depersonalization.

Delusion
A false belief which is inappropriate to an individual's socio-cultural background and which is held in the face of logical argument. True delusions commonly have a paranoid colouring (q.v.) and are held with extraordinary conviction. Delusion is thus a primary and fundamental experience in which incorrect judgements are made. The experience of delusion proper precedes its expression in words and hence, when stated, is incomprehensible and beyond argument, e.g. 'I was walking along the street and saw a dog and immediately I knew by the way it stood that I was a special person pre-destined to save mankind.'

Delusional ideas
Delusional ideas differ from true or primary delusions in that instead of arising out of the blue they occur against a background of disturbed mood and are entirely explicable in that context. Thus the severe delusional ideas of guilt and condemnation and persecution shown by a psychotic depressive are seen to be an outgrowth of the depressive state. In the same way the delusional notions of grandeur and exaltation of the manic spring from his elevated mood—a mood which brings with it breezy overconfidence and insouciance which can easily develop into ideas of omnipotence.

Flight of ideas
Accelerated thinking, characteristically seen in hypomanic and

manic illness. The association between ideas are casual, and are determined by such things as puns and rhymes. However links are detectable and the flight can be followed.

Hallucinations

A perception occurring in the absence of an outside stimulus (e.g. hearing a voice outside one). Hallucinations are particularly common in schizophrenia. Patients hear voices which tell them to do things, comment on their actions, utter obscenities or murmur wordlessly. The phenomenon of 'hearing one's thoughts spoken aloud' is encountered in schizophrenia. Hallucinations are described as hypnagogic if they are experienced whilst falling asleep and hypnopompic if experienced whilst waking up.

Hypochondriasis

Preoccupation with fancied illness. Hypochondriacal features are common in depression and may be found as bizarre phenomena in schizophrenia. Hypochondriasis may be the central feature of a hysterical illness. It seems likely that hypochondriasis does not exist on its own but is usually a manifestation of some underlying psychiatric condition or personality disorder.

Illusion

A perceptual error or misinterpretation. These commonly occur in organic mental states, particularly delirium. A patient in such a state misinterpreted a building outside his window as being a liner about to sail.

Ideas of reference

The patient who has ideas of reference experiences events and perceives objects in his environment as having a special significance for himself. For example a patient noticed that all the TV programmes she saw indicated to her in some unusual way that she had been singled out for observation by a secret police force.

Neurosis and psychosis

Although widely used the terms lack precise definition and give rise to disagreement. A working definition would be that neurotic illnesses are states in which anxiety, mild mood change and preservation of contact with reality are the rule. The neurotic patient is only too aware of his illness, and never loses contact with reality. In psychotic states, the patient loses contact with reality, there is a tendency towards the more bizarre manifestations of psychiatric disturbance as a common finding. Mood change when present is likely to be profound.

Thus it appears that we base our definitions of neurosis and psychosis on severity of symptoms rather than anything else. Such an unsatisfactory state of affairs must persist until more is known about the aetiology of psychiatric disorders in general.

Mannerism

A habitual expressive movement of the face or body. Normal mannerisms are appropriate but pathological mannerisms are inappropriate (e.g. in schizophrenia).

Obsessional phenomena (obsessive compulsive phenomena)

These are contents of consciousness of an unpleasant and recurrent sort which the patient experiences but which he resists. These contents may include words, ideas, phrases and acts. This is well exemplified by a patient who had to perform every act of washing, dressing and eating nine times or else he became anxious and distressed.

Paranoid

This is a widely known psychiatric term and about as widely misused. It derives from the Greek PARA NOUS i.e. beyond reason. It has been used for years to describe 'classic' signs of psychosis—particularly those that encompass delusions of grandeur or those of a fantastic sort.

Recent use of the term has tended to assign to it the meaning of 'persecutory', thus paranoid delusions become delusions of persecution and suspicion, oversensitive people are regarded as 'paranoid'. This is no doubt related to the fact that ideas of persecution *are* commonplace in psychosis so that by a process of condensation paranoid=psychotic=persecuted. But this is an incorrect way of using the term which should be reserved for the formal description of delusions and syndromes characterized by 'persecution, grandeur, litigation, jealousy, love, envy, hate, honour, or the supernatural' (Lewis 1970).

The term may be extended to describe the mechanism of projection by which a person refers events, even trifles, to himself, but it should be emphasized that the term implies a mechanism of psychotic intensity and not the sensitive ideas and feelings which are part of the normal experience of many.

Passivity feeling
A feeling of bodily influence or control by outside agents. This phenomenon is commonly found in schizophrenia.

Schizophrenia
A syndrome, occurring mainly in young people, in which are found characteristic disturbances of *thinking, perception, emotion* and *behaviour*. The illness tends to lead to disintegration of the personality.

Schizophrenic thought disorder
A characteristic type of disturbance of thinking, found only in schizophrenia, in which there is a basic disturbance of the process of conceptual thinking. This shows itself in the patient's speech, which reflects his impaired logical thinking. Early schizophrenic thought disorder often manifests itself as a subjective difficulty in thinking clearly. In its most severe form thought disorder reduces patients' talk to fragmented nonsense —'word salad'. Certain German psychiatrists have stressed the clinical importance of the description by a patient of the experience of feeling that thoughts are inserted into the head, or that they are being withdrawn from the head, or that one's

thoughts are being spoken aloud outside of one (Gedanken-
lauten werden). Such manifestations are usually regarded as
being of prime importance in making the diagnosis of schizophrenia.

GENERAL ADVICE REGARDING THE
EXAMINATION OF AND DESCRIPTION
OF THE MENTAL STATE

The signs of mental disturbance can be elicited provided one
learns how to do this, in much the same way that one learns to
elicit physical signs in general medicine. However, one should
avoid leading questions, and also it is important to avoid
making remarks or comments to the patient which may im-
plant in his mind disruptive or disturbing ideas. In this way
one can avoid *interpreting* to the patient the *apparent meaning* of his experiences or feelings. Interpretation should be
avoided and left to the expert. The patient should not be
antagonized if he appears to be uncooperative. Antagonism,
resistance and evasiveness can usually be overcome by handling
the situation in a non-committal way. Recording the patient's
talk verbatim is extremely useful but may antagonize a prickly
patient. Here is a scheme for the mental state:

BEHAVIOUR
In describing the patient's behaviour one should try as far as
possible to get an accurate description of how the patient
behaves during interview. One starts by observing the patient's
behaviour, instead of just taking it for granted. Points to note
include:

    (1) the patient's general level of consciousness,

    (2) awareness of what is going on around him,

    (3) his level of cooperation with the examiner,

    (4) whether he is able to make contact with the examiner
at interview,

(5) the patient's predominant facial expressions and whether they are appropriate,

(6) his use of gesture,

(7) activity—free or constrained, continuous or interrupted,

(8) the presence of agitation,

(9) use of mannerisms.

This is not a complete list but is only intended as a guide.

TALK

It is usual to consider both the *form* and the *content* of the patient's talk. The *form* is the manner of talk, i.e. how it presents, sustained, interrupted, fast or slow etc. The simplest way to examine the content of the patient's talk is by making a verbatim sample. Content means the predominant topics.

MOOD

Here we try to comment on whether the patient's mood is sustained or variable. What is the predominant mood as far as possible? Quite often a description of the patient's mood cannot be put down in one word, e.g. depressed. A useful way of enquiring about the patient's mood is to ask some questions such as 'How do you feel in yourself?' or 'How are your spirits?'

THOUGHT CONTENT

(a) *Delusions.* These can only be elicited by careful questioning. Some patients will talk very spontaneously about their delusions and express a wide variety of illogical ideas. Other patients will need to be questioned. Paranoid delusions are often persecutory and to elicit them requires bland questions which do not arouse the patient's suspicions too strongly. Such questions are 'Are people treating you as they should?' or 'How are people behaving towards you, do you suppose?' are often quite useful. Enquire about the patient's attitude to his own self. Ask whether he feels he has changed in any way, or whether he feels he is a good or bad person. This may help to elicit feelings of guilt and self-recrimination.

(b) *Hypochondriacal ideas.* It is important to recognize that hypochondriacal concern is an extremely common finding amongst psychiatric patients. Thus the anxious patient may have a considerable amount of hypochondriacal fears surrounding bodily symptoms of anxiety such as palpitations etc. On the other hand the severely depressed patient may present with severe hypochondriasis which may well be missed by the examining doctor until he is aware of the significance of hypochondriasis in depression (see Depression). Bizarre hypochondriacal notions tend to be found in schizophrenic illnesses.

(c) *Obsessive compulsive phenomena.* Here one should enquire about habits surrounding various aspects of the patient's daily life. For instance the patient with an obsessional disorder may have rituals concerned with washing and eating etc. which he feels obliged to carry out, and which occasion him much discomfiture. Very often the patient will be extremely ashamed of this type of symptom and discuss it only with difficulty.

PERCEPTUAL DISTURBANCE
Here one records hallucinations and illusions, noting the modality of the hallucination and its content. Also the occasions on which they tend to occur.

COGNITIVE TESTING
(a) *Memory.* The patient's account of his history when compared with other informants will give some assessment of his memory for past events. Recent memory may be adequately tested by asking the patient to give an account of the preceding 24 hours. The ability to retain new information and reproduce it may be tested as follows:
— give the patient a name and address and telephone number Ask him to repeat it immediately and to reproduce it in 5 minutes.

—ask the patient to listen to the Babcock sentence and repeat it, e.g. 'One thing a Nation must have to become rich and great is an adequate secure supply of wood.'

(b) *Orientation.* Record the patient's account of the time of day, date and place.

(c) *Concentration.* One should record the patient's level of attention to the questions asked him and also try and test his concentrating ability by asking him to subtract 7 from 100 until he can go no further, noting the number of mistakes and the time taken.

GENERAL INFORMATION AND INTELLIGENCE

Under the heading 'General Information' one attempts to assess the individual's store of general knowledge. Useful questions here will include such things as the patient's familiarity with current affairs, topics of the day and familiarity with reigning figures and political names. Intelligence can be assessed quite roughly clinically bearing in mind the patient's educational background and professional attainments and some attempt should be made to place a patient on the scale:

(1) below average,
(2) average,
(3) superior.

INSIGHT

Assessing the patient's insight is the most difficult thing of all. It does not merely mean asking the patient whether he knows whether he is ill or not although of course awareness of the existence of illness is an important criterion of insight. But in deciding and commenting upon the patient's level of insight, one wants to know too, how aware the patient is of the extent of his illness and its effect on other people, such as his family, employers, colleagues, etc. One wants to know too, whether the patient has any idea of how his illness seems to others or how he might feel about a similar illness in other people. Some idea about his insight might be gleaned from his views regarding future plans and so on.

SPECIAL INVESTIGATIONS

Special investigations of the mental state include the use of tests of psychological function. It is important to point out that there is no 'ideal' psychological test—a fact which surprises some students whose notions of clinical psychology are likely to be hazy. It is less than fair to clinical psychology to suppose that this is a professional discipline devoted to 'testing' psychiatric patients though psychological investigation, properly used, is used to clarify problems in diagnosis and to guide, assess and plan treatment and rehabilitation. The sophisticated use of psychological *testing* relies on the use of batteries of tests and careful selection of testing procedures by the psychologist and *not* by the doctor.

Common areas of psychiatric scrutiny include the measurement of intelligence and assessment of personality structure.

Frequently used intelligence tests include the Raven Progressive Matrices and the Mill Hill Vocabulary Scale. These are tests of general and verbal ability, are well standardized, relatively simple to administer either to individuals or groups, and give an acceptable assessment of the intelligence level. The Wechsler Adult Intelligence Scale (W.A.I.S.) is another well standardized intelligence test which is more comprehensive than the former. It includes tests of performance as well as verbal tests. Personality assessment relies first of all on the use of projective tests which are thought to reveal the subject's unconscious process e.g. the subject is asked to describe what he sees in a pattern of ink blots (Rorschach) or to make up a story about an ambiguous picture (Thematic Apperception Test).

Other methods of personality assessment include questionnaires which are designed to identify patterns of personality structure. An example of this is the M.M.P.I. (Minnesota

Multiphasic Personality Inventory). This questionnaire consists of over 500 items. The questions are designed in such a way as to tap attitudes in the respondent which may be construed as indicating in the personality the presence of elements going to make up a particular personality structure and also to reveal the presence of elements resembling at least certain clinical psychiatric syndromes.

LABORATORY INVESTIGATIONS

There are no routine investigations in psychiatric practice, although chest X-ray, skull X-ray and Wasserman are probably the most commonly used. The investigator should have some good reason for wanting to have a particular investigation done, rather than resorting to whole batteries of special investigations.

Finally the essentials of history and mental state should be summarized in a formulation of the patient's illness, giving a 'bird's eye view' of the diagnosis, likely treatment and prognosis.

REFERENCES

LEWIS A. J. (1970) Paranoia and Paranoid: a historical perspective. *Psychological Medicine*, 1, 2–12.

MAYER GROSS W., SLATER E. & ROTH M. (1960) In *Clinical Psychiatry*. Cassell, London.

STENGEL E. (1959) Classification of mental diseases. *Bull W.H.O.* 21, 601.

STEVENSON I. (1959) The psychiatric interview. In *American Handbook of Psychiatry*, vol. 1 197. Basic Books, New York.

CHAPTER 2. AFFECTIVE DISORDERS

Introduction
In the affective disorders, the primary manifestation is one of mood disturbance. This disturbance ranges from that experienced in *anxiety states* or in depression to the more profound mood disorders seen in *manic depressive psychoses*. In each case the mood disturbance is accompanied by varying psychological and physical symptoms.

Anxiety
Anxiety is a universal phenomenon in which the subject experiences a feeling *akin to fear or apprehension* usually accompanied by autonomic disturbances (sympathetic over-activity), of which the following are typical:

    (a) tachycardia and raised blood pressure,
    (b) palpitations,
    (c) dryness of mouth,
    (d) diarrhoea, epigastric discomfort, nausea,
    (e) dilated pupils,
    (f) sweating,
    (g) frequency of micturition,
    (h) headache.

Despite its universality, not all anxiety is pathological. It is useful to distinguish between *healthy* and *morbid* anxiety.

Healthy anxiety is experienced by most people under un-accustomed *stress*—examinations, interviews etc., being typical examples. It is a normal response to an unusual situation, an *adaptive response* on the part of the organism which prepares him for a task or ordeal requiring further effort and making unusual demands on him.

17

Morbid anxiety, however, is different; it is an *unadaptive response* and serves no useful purpose, once it is established—quite the opposite in fact! Too often it pervades the mental life of the individual and becomes a rein not a spur. The morbidly anxious patient is soon aware of the *paradoxical nature* of his affliction. Anxiety is experienced both in the presence of or the absence of what can be seen to be obvious stimuli. The patient knows that his fears are irrational and groundless but this is no help to him as he magnifies, scrutinizes and mulls over the content of his anxiety.

Aetiology

I. AGE

Anxiety is most common in adolescence and old age. *Adolescence* can be and often is a time of stress and turmoil. Young people are subject to all sorts of pressures at this time of their lives. Normal adolescent development is a period during which strong emotions are easily aroused—emotions which the subject finds hard to channel. He is at an 'in between' stage of life where he is accorded neither adult nor childish status. He is often oversensitive and prickly, particularly about his appearance which is more often than not gauche and pimply. It is hardly surprising then that emergent sexuality is tantalized by advertisements extolling the virtues of flawless skin or correct bust size. The adolescent is full of doubts about himself—will he get a job—the right sort of job? Will he get into a university? Is he going to be socially, sexually and in every other way competent when put to the test? All these sorts of questions are in his mind and it seems to him that everyone offers conflicting advice. In this setting he may develop *anxiety symptoms*, usually of an acute sort.

Often the anxiety symptoms of the adolescent may find their most extreme expression in a near psychotic breakdown—sometimes mistakenly diagnosed as schizophrenia—which has been called the *adolescent crisis of identity*. This syndrome is really what the name suggests, a state in which the youngster becomes so uncertain of himself and his role that he breaks down into an overwhelming state of anxious uncertainty where contact with reality may apparently be lost. A good fictional description of this is to be found in the novel *Catcher in the Rye* by J. D. Salinger.

The adolescent crisis of identity usually responds well to straightforward and sympathetic management. It is important that such patients are not mistakenly *labelled* as schizophrenic; on the other hand it has to be remembered that schizophrenia is a state which can and does begin in adolescence. But in schizophrenia the evidence for a more profound process should be sought for, personality change, thought disorder etc. (See schizophrenia.)

Sources of anxiety in adolescence then are common; they may be personal, social or cultural. The symptom itself needs investigation and treatment since adolescence is a time of change and maturation. Sensible handling in adolescence may help the individual avoid chronicity of symptoms and the carry over of unresolved adolescent problems in adult life.

Old age. Elderly people readily become anxious when the orderly routine of their life is threatened. Loneliness and the fear of death are also important causes of anxiety in old age. Often the anxieties of the elderly may be too readily dismissed as if they were of little significance because the patient is *old*. As if old age were necessarily a sort of laissez passer to wretchedness which it need not be though too often is.

2. CONSTITUTION

Some people are, by nature, more anxious than others. From early years and throughout their lives they are insecure, timid, and emotionally unstable. Their fears are easily aroused and they are over fussy about their health—tending readily towards hypochondriasis. Their *work records* are *poor*, and they show a *low level* of *drive, energy, ambition* and *persistence*. This combination of traits is regarded as evidence of *constitutional neuroticism* and the evidence for its existence has been convincingly demonstrated (Slater, Rees & Eysenck). Neuroticism correlates highly with physique, vasomotor instability and a background of poor general health.

3. LEARNING

There is much experimental evidence to suggest that where anxiety is linked to *specific stressors* (cats, open spaces etc.) the *phobia* as it is called, is a learned phenomenon, i.e. has been developed by a process of simple conditioning and is subject to the same laws (generalization, inhibition, extinction etc.). This has been exploited therapeutically by using processes of *de-conditioning* to extinguish *phobias* (see treatment).

Clinical Picture of Anxiety

In addition to experiencing the specific manifestations described at the beginning of this section, anxious patients often complain of feelings of *tension*, or of difficulty in *concentrating*. Tension manifests itself not only by a 'feeling of being strung up' but also by heaviness or pains in the limbs.

Associated *mood change of depressive type* is very commonly associated with anxiety—in fact a state of anxiety in pure culture is extremely rare—sooner or later depression appears.

Other bodily accompaniments of anxiety include decreased libido and impotence. Sleep is poor—typically the patient finds it hard to get off to sleep and may experience broken sleep throughout the night when he will tend to wake and lie awake worrying about his fears.

Anxiety states may present to the doctor in a wide range of symptoms involving almost every system of the body: The cardiologist may be consulted about palpitations; the chest physician about difficulty in breathing; the gastro-enterologist about dyspepsia and the neurologist about weakness and headaches. So, that the bodily manifestations of anxiety are likely to be those of which the patient complains—since they are what make him feel unwell. While careful investigation is a part of all medical care it has to be realized that in the treatment of the patient with anxiety that investigation carried to excess may reinforce the disorder. So that the doctor has to strike a balance between over-investigation and inadequate reassurance and under investigation with over confident reassurance.

Diagnosis

Simple states of anxiety uncomplicated by depression are uncommon—most anxious patients have some depressive mood change. Anxiety may be prominent in the onset of a depressive illness. It is also not uncommon to find anxiety in the early stages of schizophrenia. Before deciding that a patient is suffering from simple anxiety one has to exclude:

(1) depression,
(2) schizophrenia.

However episodic attacks which can be confused with anxiety can be caused by:

(a) temporal lobe epilepsy,
(b) adrenalin secreting tumours,
(c) hypoglycaemia.

Treatment

A. PHYSICAL

(1) *Sedation*

Sedation, either with barbiturates or tranquillizers will relieve the symptoms of anxiety in the first instance, useful drugs include.

(a) *Sedatives*. Amytal 30-100 mg t.d.s.

Barbiturates have recently lost their previously impeccable medical credentials because of their overprescription by an irresponsible minority of doctors for an irresponsible minority of patients. Barbiturates are useful sedatives as long as they are used only for short periods. Many patients get good subjective relief from them. The trouble is that it is easy to become dependent. Phenobarbitone should be avoided as it causes depression.

c

(b) *Tranquillizers.* The main tranquillizers used to relieve anxiety symptoms are the Benzodiazepines, viz.

Chlordiazepoxide (Librium)	up to 60 mg daily
Diazepam (Valium)	up to 60 mg daily
Oxazepam (Serenid)	up to 90 mg daily.

The tranquillizers or 'anxiolytic' drugs are, strictly speaking, tranquillosedative drugs and have some abuse potential. If taken in excessive doses they produce states of chronic intoxication, i.e. drowsiness, dysarthria and ataxia and also withdrawal fits if the drug is stopped.

(2) *Modified Insulin Treatment*

Small doses of insulin sufficient to induce hypoglycaemic hunger and drowsiness are useful in treating the anxious patient, particularly if anorexia and weight loss are a problem. This form of treatment is usually given to in-patients and day patients but can equally well be given to out-patients.

The dose is given in the morning. The subject is given increasing doses of soluble insulin each day till a dosage level is reached which induces a drowsy relaxed state. After three hours he has a hearty breakfast and glucose drink.

B. PSYCHOLOGICAL

Psychological treatment of anxiety is of two sorts:

> psychotherapy,
> behaviour therapy.

(1) *Psychotherapy*

Psychotherapy aims to relieve anxiety by discovering causes in the patient's unconscious mental life, by solving problems and resolving conflict. There are many schools of psychotherapy (e.g. Freudian and Jungian), but all subscribe to the belief that behaviour is controlled by unconscious forces and emotion rather than by reason.

The simplest form of psychotherapy is *supportive.* In this the doctor listens and permits the patient to ventilate his feelings and arrive at solutions of problems without guidance or interpretation. The role of the doctor is to provide unbiased sympathy and encouragement.

Analytic psychotherapy aims at exploration of the unconscious. It is necessarily a lengthy process. The most suitable subjects are people with above average intelligence and good verbal ability. The two most widely known schools of analytic psychotherapy are Freudian and Jungian Analysis. All psychotherapeutic methods acknowledge the fundamental importance of the relationship that exists between patient and doctor in psychotherapy. This relationship can vary from one extreme to another as the patient invests the doctor with every sort of emotion. The trained psychotherapist accepts this relationship and handles it as part of the therapeutic process. The patient transfers to the doctor, emotions which previously he had experienced about key figures in his personality development. This is called 'the transference'.

(2) *Behaviour Therapy*

When anxiety is linked to specific stresses (e.g. cats, heights, open spaces) and only triggered off by these, it is called *phobic anxiety*. These phobias may be single or multiple.

In recent years, psychologists studying theories of learning have pointed out that phobias are probably the result of maladaptive learning i.e. the patient has become conditioned to experience anxiety at the sight or sound of a given object. They have reasoned from this that the phobias could be cured by a deconditioning process which desensitizes the patient from the cause of the attacks. This has the advantage of being based on a rational theoretical basis. The most obvious drawback appears to be that its usefulness is limited by the fact that it is only applicable to patients with isolated phobias.

Behaviour therapy has been criticized for the failure to take into account the existence of a therapeutic relationship between doctor and patient and its consequent effects in altering the course of the patient's illness. However, more careful evaluation of behaviour therapeutic methods has shown that this need not necessarily be the case.

In general it may be said that the term behaviour therapy is applied to a variety of psychiatric treatment in which use is made of the principles of behavioural sciences in re-educating a patient away from abnormal behaviour.

The theoretical basis runs counter to a dynamic basis in that it rejects the supposed importance of unconscious processes and conflict, stressing rather the importance of symptoms as learnt manifestations of a neurotic disorder.

The beginning of behaviour therapy occurred in the early 1950's when Professor H. J. Eysenck and colleagues in the Institute of Psychiatry in London made serious criticisms of the value of conventional psychotherapy and suggested in its stead the use of behaviour therapy a treatment in which learnt neurotic responses would be replaced using learning and de-conditioning techniques.

Typical methods of behaviour therapy include
    (a) conditioned avoidance,
    (b) reciprocal inhibition,
    (c) desensitization.

(a) *Conditioned avoidance*

In these techniques the behaviour to be extinguished—e.g. alcoholism, sexual deviation, is linked to an aversive stimulus such as apomorphine causing nausea thus producing in the subject a state of conditioned aversion.

(b) *Reciprocal inhibition*

This technique is based on the finding that some human behaviours are mutually exclusive e.g. relaxation and tension. In practice use is made of this finding by endeavouring to replace an unwanted response by one which is incompatible with it. In time the subject responds with relaxation to situations which have previously caused fear.

(c) *Desensitization*

Here the subject learns to avoid responding to noxious stimuli by being exposed to the stimuli at such minimal levels that little or no unpleasant response occurs. In this way his tolerance to the stimuli improves and the response is lost.

(d) *Flooding*

A newer technique in behaviour therapy is 'Flooding' or 'implosion' in which the patient is not desensitized from the dreaded stimulus but brought face to face with it until the anxiety fades. It sounds terrible but it works!

DEPRESSION

In depression the mood resembles sadness or grief but is sustained, unlike the transitory mood changes that many people experience in response to various stresses, or from one part of the day to the other. The important thing about depressive states is that this change of mood is sustained and that it exceeds quantitatively and qualitatively these ordinary variations. In addition there are other bodily and emotional disturbances. There is no point in expanding the concept of depression in an attempt to explain away every variety of human unhappiness.

It is often hard to distinguish 'true' depression from states of unhappy malaise that trouble people with abnormal personalities, those who abuse drugs or alcohol or for that matter people with chronic painful illnesses. These are more than unhappiness, yet they are not depression—often they are referred to as states of 'dysphoria'.

The accompaniments of depression are:

    (1) insomnia,
    (2) loss of energy,
    (3) loss of interest,
    (4) anorexia,

(5) weight loss,

(6) decreased libido and impotence.

Depressions are often described either as being *reactive* or *endogenous*. Since these terms are in such common use some explanation must be made of them but it is a fact that their *use is controversial*.

Reactive depression is usually so named if the depression can be shown to satisfy the following conditions.

(1) Its onset follows some obvious cause in the patient's life such as loss of a job, broken engagement, examination failure etc.

(2) The content of the illness is concerned with the cause to the exclusion of everything else.

(3) The illness would not have come on if the precipitating event had not occurred.

Endogenous depression is so named if:

(1) The depression arises out of the blue, unrelated to external events.

(2) There is diurnal variation of mood.

(3) There is sleep disturbance with early morning waking. In practice the distinction between these two 'types' of depression is hard to make—what at first sight appears to be 'reactive' depression then turns out to be endogenous by virtue of the presence of diurnal mood variation, early waking etc.

Aetiology

I. HEREDITY

The incidence of manic depressive psychosis in the population is somewhere in the region of 1 per cent. Family studies of depressive patients show an incidence of depression in about 11 per cent of the relatives as a whole. Broken down the incidence of depression in the relatives of depressive patients is as follows:

Sibs 23 per cent.

Half sibs 17 per cent.

The type of genetic transmission is not known. A multi-factorial inheritance is the most likely. However, depressive states of lesser severity are common and it has been estimated that in a practice of 2,000 patients, the General Practitioner may expect to encounter around 12 new cases in a year. (Watts)

2. SEX
Depression is more common in women than men.

3. RACE
Affective disorders are in general described as being more common in Jews and in the Irish than in other races.

4. SOCIAL CLASS
Though it is generally held that affective disorders are more common in Social Classes I and II of the population, in contrast to schizophrenia which is more common in Social Classes IV and V, it should be remembered that more subtle social factors may operate at least to some extent. In the 'upper' social classes depression may be more likely to be recognized by patient and doctor. That this can be the case in America, at any rate, was shown by Holinshed and Redlich who demonstrated that diagnosis and treatment were materially affected by membership of a particular social class. Upper class people were found to be more likely to be diagnosed as neurotic and receive psychotherapy while lower class people were more likely to be diagnosed as psychotic and receive E.C.T. And these biases appeared to be determined by social class.

5. CONSTITUTION
(a) *Body Type*. The body type is more predominantly 'pyknic', i.e. small extremities and large visceral cavities (Mr Pickwick).

(b) *Personality*. A personality type notable for swings of mood 'cyclothymic' personality is a common accompaniment of affective disorder.

Many patients who develop *mania* have a premorbid personality notable for unusual jollity and energy—the so-called hypomanic personality.

6. STRESS

The relationship of depression to apparent external causes is often obscure and misleading—causes invoked by patient or relative may be no more than an expression of the illness itself. For example a man presented with a history of depression after dismissal from his job. On closer questioning it became clear that his symptoms of depression had antedated his sacking and that he had lost his job because of his incompetence, itself a manifestation of depression.

7. AGE

Age plays a part in the aetiology of depression, some age groups being particularly vulnerable. Old age with loneliness and the fear of death is the most obvious example. Middle age can be particularly threatening, particularly for the striving man who suddenly arrives at this age and realizes he has accomplished less than he hoped. If this coincides with the loss of his children by marriage etc., it is liable to be all the harder to bear and frank depression may develop. Adolescence is a time of turmoil and depression at this age, though rare, when it does occur is severe.

8. PHYSIOLOGICAL EVENTS PRECIPITATING DEPRESSION

(a) *Childbirth is the first and most obvious example*—an event of physiological and psychological significance. Lability of mood is normal in the puerperium but acute severe depression does occur and needs prompt recognition and treatment.

(b) The *menopause* is a time of hormonal and psychological change and is often accompanied by depression.

(c) *Acute febrile illnesses* such as influenza can trigger off depression.

(d) *Chronic illness*, particularly chronic *painful* illness is commonly accompanied by depression. Unfortunately this depression often passes unrecognized since such depression can be relieved and the illness made more easy to bear.

(e) *Jaundice.*

9. SOCIAL FACTORS

Social isolation and insecurity with loneliness and accompanying despair probably account for a large proportion of chronic depression.

10. DRUGS

(a) Reserpine.

(b) Certain anti-parkinsonian agents e.g. Benzhexol may cause depression or states of excitement.

Manifestations of Depression

1. MOOD CHANGE

Mood change is fundamental in every depressive illness. Here it is worth noting that one should not confuse the lay and medical usage of the term 'depression'. When we talk of depression we refer to a *clinical entity* and do not use it loosely to describe transitory feelings of sadness or dejection.

The depressed patient's mood colours his entire mental life; thus in severe depression he will form incorrect judgements— delusional ideas based on his altered mood—e.g. saying that he has been condemned to death for his numerous misdeeds.

Such severe depression is not common, what is much more common is a general depressive colouring to the patient's outlook. The world seems grey and dark to him, his future appears grim and he sees himself as a failure, unworthy of anyone's pity or affection. People who feel like this are likely to attempt suicide. Ideas of guilt and unworthiness are extremely common in depression.

2. PSYCHOMOTOR ACTIVITY

Alteration in psychomotor activity follows in the wake of mood change. The patient's movements and talk are slow and ponderous. This is called *retardation*. The patient is aware of this and often describes slowness in thought and difficulty in concentration. These latter can be elicited by simple tests of concentration such as the serial subtraction of seven from one hundred.

Poor concentration shows itself in the patient's work or studies and is confirmed by colleagues who tell one that he is not coping as well with his work as formerly. The housewife finds that work piles up in the home whilst she sits around in a hopeless state unable to concentrate but feeling sad and dejected. Frank weeping is not particularly common in depression. Far more common is the statement 'I've got past the stage of being able to cry. I can't cry any more. Perhaps I'd feel better if I could.'

3. SLEEP DISTURBANCE
Insomnia is very common in depression and may be manifest as delayed sleep, broken sleep or early waking. Early waking is said to be the most common form of persistent sleep disorder. The patient wakes in the early hours and is unable to sleep thereafter he remains awake for a few hours till he gets up unrefreshed. Often he has bad dreams.

4. OTHER BODILY DISTURBANCES
By day the patient lacks energy, interest and appetite. Weight loss is common. Apathy and loss of interest may be the presenting symptoms of depression. Hypochondriacal concern is commonly found, particularly centring on the bowels which are often constipated.

5. OTHER PSYCHOLOGICAL ACCOMPANIMENTS
Anxiety is encountered in almost every depressive illness—there is no point in attempting clinical separation of anxiety from depression. Elderly depressed patients usually show *agitation* that is to say restless semi-purposive overactivity with hand wringing and inability to sit or lie still. Agitation can

sometimes be so severe as to resemble manic excitement except that the affect is one of hopelessness and despair. *Paranoid features,* particularly in middle aged and elderly patients may dominate the clinical picture in depression.

Hysterical symptoms can either mask depression or complicate the picture. In the first instance failure to recognize the essential depressive nature of the illness can be very dangerous particularly when the hysterical symptom is protecting the patient from a suicidal impulse.

Hypochondriasis is extremely common in depressive states—in its most severe form one finds hypochondriacal delusions in the severely depressed patient, more common perhaps is the finding of a pervasive hypochondriacal attitude in the concern about the bodily accompaniments of depression such as constipation etc. Very often this hypochondriasis is the presenting symptom of depression and may bring the patient initially to the attention of an investigating physician rather than a psychiatrist.

Differential Diagnosis of Depression
Important physical disorders to be excluded are:

(a) *Myxoedema.* Remembering that in myxoedema, depression and paranoid psychoses are commonly manifestations of the underlying disorder.

(b) *Parkinsonism.* Depression is a common accompaniment of Parkinsonism.

(c) *Myasthenia Gravis.*

(d) *Addison's Disease.*

The important psychiatric conditions to be distinguished from depression are:

(a) *Schizophrenia.* Though the presence of thought disorder and true delusions may make the diagnosis of schizophrenia on occasions comparatively simple it has to be remembered that the prodroma of schizophrenia may be apparently entirely depressive, hence adolescent depression should be diagnosed very cautiously.

(b) *Dementia*. Presence of signs of organic deterioration should make diagnosis of dementia possible though atypical depressions may simulate dementia and depression may complicate dementia.

Complications of Depression

1. Suicide and attempted suicide. All depressed patients should be carefully assessed for the possibility of suicide. Threats should never be ignored and must always be carefully evaluated. It is very important always to remember that there are a number of rather foolish statements about suicide which have been made which must be disregarded. First of these is 'if a patient talks about suicide they won't do it', nothing could be further from the truth. There are some generally agreed pointers which may indicate an impending suicidal attempt and they include severe sleep disturbance with increased concern about it; history of previous suicidal attempt; a family history of suicide; suicidal talk and preoccupation; severe hypochondriasis; associated physical illness; social isolation, persistent feelings of guilt and self-depreciation.

In recent years the taking of tablets in the form of deliberate overdosage has become so common in hospital practice that some have suggested that the term attempted suicide for these people should be discarded and that this should be referred to as self-poisoning. At all events whatever the condition is called it should always be remembered that from time to time people will take sleeping pills etc. in doses in excess of the therapeutic level in an attempt to blot out reality by deep sleep and also as a way of drawing attention to their personal or social problems. This is not to suggest that all suicidal attempts constitute a serious psychiatric emergency but rather that every one of these attempts should be evaluated by the physician with careful regard to the individual's personal and social situation.

2. Malnutrition.

3. Worsening of co-existing physical disease through neglect etc., e.g. Pulmonary Tuberculosis, Diabetes Mellitus.

4. Abuse of drugs or alcohol in an attempt to 'fight off' depression.

Treatment

Of all psychiatric disorders depression is the most treatable. Nowadays the majority of depressives are treated as out-patients but admission to hospital will always be necessary for severe depression, particularly where there is suicidal risk.

METHODS OF TREATMENT

1. *General Measures*

In the present era of physical treatments the possibility of spontaneous remission is not awaited since most psychiatrists rightly feel that the patient's suffering should not be needlessly prolonged.

However it should be remembered that good psychiatric nursing and sedation will always provide comfort and some degree of improvement to the depressed patient.

2. *Physical Treatment*

(a) *Electro-convulsive therapy* (*E.C.T.*). E.C.T. has come to be regarded as almost specific antidepressive treatment (see Chapter 11). It is usually given twice or three times per week —on the average 8–10 treatments will produce remission of the depressive illness.

(b) *Anti-depressive drugs* including:

Amitryptiline (Tryptizole)
25–50 mg t.d.s.
Imipramine (Tofranil)
25–50 mg t.d.s. } Imino dibenzyl derivatives

and Isocarboxazid (Marplan)
10–20 mg t.d.s. } Monoamine oxidase inhibitor

(c) *Psychotherapy.* Usually supportive.

(d) *Occupational therapy.*

(e) *Social rehabilitation.*

Prognosis

Depression tends to recur. It may well be that prolonged medication with anti-depressive drugs helps to avert recurrence, though it is too early to be definite about this. The average duration of hospitalization in depression is about six weeks.

MANIA

Mania is less common than depression and tends to be an acute and more circumscribed illness. Chronic depression is commonplace—chronic mania does not exist.

Hypomania is the term used to describe mild or moderate degrees of mania.

Aetiology

(1) See depression.

(2) *Premorbid personality.* Commonly the manic patient is found to have either a cyclothymic personality or else to have always been more energetic and cheerful than his fellows (*hypomanic personality*).

Manifestations

MOOD

The mood is one of cheerfulness—or hilarity. Manic patients are described as showing *infectious jollity*—soon everyone in the room is laughing with them. This is often true, but the jollity is more often than not well laced with irritability and flashes of anger, particularly if someone disagrees with the patient. The manic patient denies all symptoms and says he has never felt better in his life. He is optimistic and has elaborate plans for the future, not only his future but for anyone else who cares to take advantage of the plans he is making. The plans at first may be sensible, if a little over-enthusiastically stated but sooner or later they become grandiose as the patient's *critical sense* fades. The patient's *insight* about his lack of judgement is practically nil in mania. Sudden mood changes with transient bouts of tearful sadness are also encountered.

ACTIVITY

The overactivity in mania follows naturally from the feeling of general well being that the patient experiences. His energy is boundless. He gets up before everyone else in the house and goes to bed long after exhausted members of the family have retired. At work he goes from one project to another, completing nothing. He overspends, buys all sorts of things, dresses extravagantly and invites large numbers of unexpected friends home. As activity increases so the patient's *attention* decreases so that he is able to concentrate less on anything.

TALK

Talk reflects the cheery mood and increased activity. The stream of talk gradually increases till it becomes torrential. It flits from topic to topic (flight of ideas), and associations are casual, often triggered by rhymes or puns. Jokes are frequent.

DELUSIONS

True delusions are not found but the manic patient does form delusional ideas based on his overoptimistic views of life in general. It is also not uncommon to find the *irritable manic* showing a *paranoid attitude*, particularly when any objections are made to his plans.

BODILY DISTURBANCE

Sleep is lost through excessive energy.
Appetite is often voracious without any weight gain.
Libido is heightened.
Abuse of alcohol is common.

Mode of Onset

Onset is usually acute and the duration of a manic illness is on the average about 6–8 weeks.

Hypomania often passes unrecognized at first, it is merely remarked by relatives that the patient had seemed full of zest and cheeriness for a few weeks and then things seemed to get out of hand.

Some manic illnesses terminate abruptly, others swing into depression.

DIAGNOSIS

(1) Schizophrenic and schizo-affective psychoses. The presence of true thought disorder and delusions should make simple the diagnosis of these from mania. In practice it is often difficult to be precise about states of excitement. Time usually clarifies the picture.

(2) Drug induced excitement, e.g. amphetamine and its derivatives.

Treatment

(1) ADMISSION TO HOSPITAL

(2) ATTENTION TO FEEDING ETC.

The manic patient may be so overactive that he stops eating for a few days before admission. This means that he arrives in hospital exhausted and dehydrated. As a consequence his mental state may be the more disturbed through vitamin depletion.

(3) MEDICATION

(a) *Sedatives.* Immediate sedation to calm a wildly excited patient can be used but this has generally been replaced by the use of tranquillizers.

(b) *Tranquillizers.* Tranquillizers are extremely useful in calming manic excitement though whether they actually shorten a manic illness is questionable. Commonly used are:

(1) Chlorpromazine: up to 1 g per 24 h. in divided doses,

(2) Thioridazine (Melleril),

(3) Haloperidol: initially 6 mg b.d. reduced to 3 mg b.d. as soon as a calming effect is noticed. Extra-pyramidal side effects commonly occur with this drug. They can be well controlled with anti-parkinsonian medication.

(4) E.C.T. E.C.T. has a definite place in the treatment of mania. It is usually given with tranquillizers.

(5) Lithium. Lithium was first recognized as a psychotropic drug as long ago as 1897, had a bad reputation for toxicity until 1949 when interest in its use was revived. Present uses are (a) treatment of acute manic states, (b) treatment of recurrent manic states, (c) treatment of chronic depressive states. In the case of acute mania it appears to have a definite place, though its value in recurrent mania i.e. as a prophylactic drug is less certain. Its place in the treatment of chronic depression is very uncertain. The drug is given as lithium carbonate, usually at a dose of 300–600 mg t.d.s. levelling off to a lower maintenance dose. Its toxic effects necessitate frequent monitoring of the serum lithium level which should not rise above 1·6 to 1·9 mEql. Toxic effects include

- (a) gastro-intestinal effects—anorexia, nausea, vomiting and diarrhoea,
- (b) neuromuscular effects—weakness, tremor, ataxia and choreoathetosis,
- (c) C.N.S. effects—incontinence, dysarthria, blurred vision, dizziness, fits, retardation, somnolence and confusion, stupor, coma,
- (d) cardiovascular effects—pulse irregularities, E.C.G. changes, circulatory collapse.

Other effects: polyuria, polydipsia, dehydration.

Because of its toxicity lithium should not be given to any one with any degree of renal impairment. And in general it is a drug that should only be used in the setting of in-patient and out-patient hospital care.

Conclusion

In general of the affective disorders it can be said that depression is a common disorder which is amenable to treatment by a wide variety of methods and is one which can cause a great deal of hardship, and for this reason should not pass unrecognized. In the treatment of depression a good rule to abide by is that if the patient is not showing improvement with a particular line of treatment this line of treatment should not be pushed to the level of absurdity before trying something else.

REFERENCES

FREUD S. (1936) *The Problem of Anxiety.* Norton, New York.

FREUD S. (1959) Mourning and melancholia. In *Collected Papers,* vol. 4. Basic Books, New York.

HORNEY K. (1937) *The Neurotic Personality of Our Time.* Norton, New York.

KILOH L. & GARSIDE R. F. (1963) Independence of neurotic depression and endogenous depression. *Brit. J. Psychiat.* **109**, 451.

KLEIN M. (1950) *Contributions to Psycho Analysis.* Hogarth, London.

KRAEPELIN E. (1921) *Manic Depressive Insanity and Paranoia.* Livingstone, Edinburgh.

LEWIS A. J. (1934) Melancholia. A clinical survey of depressive states. *J. Ment. Sci.* **80**, 277.

MEYER V. & CRISP A. H. 1966 'Some Problems in Behaviour Therapy'. *Brit. J. Psychiat.* **112**, 367/381.

REES L. (1950) Body size, personality and neurosis. *J. Ment. Sci.* **96**, 168.

REES L. & EYSENCK H. J. (1945) A factorial study of some morphological and psychological aspects of human constitution. *J. Ment. Sci.* **91**, 8.

SLATER E. (1943) The Neurotic Constitution. *J. Neurol. Psychiat.* **6**, 1.

WATTS C. A. H. (1966) *Depressive Disorders in the Community.* John Wright, Bristol.

CHAPTER 3. SCHIZOPHRENIA

Definition
Schizophrenia is a syndrome in which are found specific psychological manifestations recognizable clinically, occurring in younger age groups and commonly leading to disintegration of the personality. The schizophrenic has peculiar ways of thinking and behaving and perceives his environment in an abnormal way. He has an inner life dominated by fantastic ideas, his emotional display is incongruous and he is cut off from his fellows so that he appears to have withdrawn from the world. The syndrome was originally described by Kraepelin (1896) who delineated its essentials under the name 'Dementia Praecox'. This was a fundamental step in the history of descriptive psychiatry since up till that time what we now recognize as schizophrenia was buried in a multitude of apparently dissimilar syndromes. The name 'Schizophrenia' was applied by Bleuler who viewed the syndrome as being based on a process of psychological disintegration manifesting itself ultimately as a fragmentation of the personality.

Aetiology
1. INCIDENCE
The incidence of schizophrenia is found to be 0·85 per cent of the general population. This figure is remarkably constant whatever populations are surveyed.

2. HEREDITY
The precise role of heredity in schizophrenia is uncertain and the means of inheritance unknown. It is possible to calculate the expectancy of schizophrenia in the family of a schizo-

phrenic where the incidence in the proband's parents may be between 5 and 10 per cent and in full sibs 5–15 per cent. Twin studies used to be quoted as showing a concordance rate of up to 80 per cent in monozygotic twins but the figure is now said to be 60 per cent, though some put the figure as low as 30 per cent. Schizophrenia breeds true in families; on the other hand 60 per cent of schizophrenics have no family history.

3. PERSONALITY

Many writers have stressed the importance of the pre-morbid personality structure of the schizophrenic. As ever one is confronted with the difficulty of assessing personality but even so a 'schizoid personality' has been described. This is a personality type which can be seen to contain the seeds of schizophrenia. Schizoid individuals display behavioural traits such as seclusiveness, abnormal shyness, hypochondriasis, emotional coolness and indifference, fanaticism and eccentricity. However there is some difference found by various workers in the incidence of these abnormal personalities before the onset of schizophrenia. M. Bleuler found a 34 per cent incidence of schizoid personality in a series of schizophrenics. Other workers have found a higher incidence but it has to be admitted that up to 50 per cent of schizophrenics show no evidence of previous personality disorder. Nevertheless the finding of personality disorder in an individual suspected of the slow development of schizophrenia may be a useful pointer toward the diagnosis. Further evidence of the role played by personality abnormality in the aetiology of schizophrenia is demonstrated by the increased incidence of deviant individuals in the families of schizophrenics.

4. BODY-BUILD

The incidence of the asthenic body structure has been commented on by many workers. This type of body-build is of poor prognostic significance—tending to be associated with chronicity.

5. CHILDHOOD EXPERIENCE

Important theories of family processes in the aetiology of schizophrenia are the 'double bind theory' of Bateson and that of Lidz and Associates.

Bateson has postulated a family situation in which the young child is constantly threatened by a parent who bombards him with inappropriate commands containing implied negatives i.e. ordering the child to disobey the orders given.

In this situation the victim can expect punishment whatever he does: moreover he may expect punishment if he makes no choice and takes no action. The theory extrapolates from this to a situation where the child learns to avoid punishment by making meaningless remarks and comes to behave as if he can no longer understand others, i.e. becomes schizophrenic.

Lidz and co-workers postulate the importance of a family situation in which the family as a whole displays pathological patterns of thought, behaviour and view of the world in general.

R. D. Laing has pointed out that a family may pressurize a member into a psychotic position by ensnaring him in a net of ambiguity, which leaves him no alternative but to act in a way that may seem odd or 'psychotic' but is actually the victim's only way of self-preservation in a malign family situation.

It is difficult to evaluate these theories of schizophrenic aetiology but it should not be thought that their explanatory and speculative nature makes them in any way mutually exclusive as compared with biological theories. Far from it. Schizophrenia is a heterogeneous collection of syndromes and no unitary theory of causality is acceptable on the evidence presently available.

6. ENDOCRINE AND METABOLIC STUDIES

These have been exhaustive and for the most part unrewarding though there is a growing body of evidence to suggest that the disturbance of schizophrenia may be biochemically transmitted. The precise nature of this disturbance is as yet unknown. The use of hallucinogenic drugs such as lysergic acid diethylamide and mescaline have induced so-called 'model psychoses' in volunteers. In these biochemically induced psychoses workers have seen resemblances to schizophrenia, and it has been argued from this that the schizophrenic psychosis is biochemically determined. This line of enquiry may become more productive when more is known about brain function than at present.

At the present time it has to be admitted that though many seemingly promising lines of enquiry of a biochemical sort have been opened in recent years—each has proved to be ultimately misleading. The position has been carefully reviewed by Kety (1965) who was able to draw the somewhat general depressing conclusion that although there was compelling evidence for the presence of genetic and biological factors in the aetiology of schizophrenia the identification of these factors was as yet well-nigh impossible A popular hypothesis is that the schizophrenic's brain may produce an abnormal central transmitting substance under stress. This causes symptoms which induce further stress and thus set up a self-perpetuating psychotic state.

7. PHYSICAL ILLNESS
Physical happenings such as illnesses, operations or accidents can commonly precipitate an acute schizophrenic psychosis or bring about remission in an established one.

8. LIFE CHANGES
Recent research suggests that schizophrenic onset and relapse are significantly preceded by life changes such as moving house, loss of a job, bereavement etc. The implication of this may be that the schizophrenic has a low tolerance for change or over-stimulation.

9. PSYCHOLOGICAL FACTORS
The role of psychological factors in the aetiology of schizophrenia is far from clear. Common clinical experience teaches

us that the schizophrenic may have the illness triggered off by any variety of psychological stress.

A comprehensive theory of the aetiology of schizophrenia would postulate that the schizophrenic process is mediated biochemically i.e. follows a biochemical final common path, that the illness occurs in a genetically pre-disposed individual, and that this disturbance may be triggered off by a variety of physical or psychological stresses or both. It would certainly seem at the present time that this theory of multiple aetiology would be the most profitable one to follow in research.

Schizophrenia therefore, appears to be a complex disturbance occurring at many levels in which hereditary, psychological, neurophysiological, sociological and biochemical factors may all play relevant parts.

Manifestations of Schizophrenia
These are best considered under the following headings:

    (a) thought disorder,
    (b) delusions,
    (c) emotional disturbance,
    (d) perceptual disturbance,
    (e) behavioural disturbance.

The reason for commencing with thought disorder lies in the fact that Bleuler in his original description of schizophrenia stressed the central position of the disturbance of thinking found in schizophrenia.

(a) SCHIZOPHRENIC THOUGHT DISORDER
This is a characteristic disturbance of the thought process peculiar to the schizophrenic syndrome. The schizophrenic's powers of thinking are impaired i.e. his powers of *conceptual thinking are altered*, so that he may interchange cause and effect and draw entirely illogical conclusions from false premises. This will manifest itself by the finding that his talk is difficult to follow. When one examines an example of this talk one finds that the patient has said much but got little across.

Closer examination reveals he has uttered a stream of nonsense. Subjectively the patient may be aware of impaired thinking ability and may tell the examiner that he finds it hard to think clearly or that his thoughts are vague, or that he cannot concentrate, or that somehow his thoughts wander. It may be necessary to use leading questions to elicit this information from a patient. As thought disorder is manifest in language, it has been suggested that the schizophrenic is forced to construct for himself a private language to explain his illogical ideas to himself and others.

Attention is often drawn to the phenomenon of *thought blocking*. Here on the patient's stream of thought is interrupted, and a new line of thinking begins. It is shown by gaps in the patient's talk and found too in states of exhaustion and depressive retardation. Thought blocking is therefore *not peculiar to schizophrenia*. All the foregoing comments on schizophrenic thought disorder presuppose that the individual is of adequate intelligence. The diagnosis of schizophrenic thought disorder in the presence of sub-normal intelligence would be extremely difficult.

The schizophrenic may experience interruption of thinking and tell the examiner that his *thoughts are being withdrawn* (thought withdrawal) from his head, or that thoughts are being inserted into his head. This sort of complaint is absolutely diagnostic of schizophrenia and occurs in no other condition. In addition he may experience transmission of his own thoughts to others. The term 'schizophrenic thought disorder' refers to the *specific disturbance of conceptual thinking* mentioned at the beginning of this section.

(b) DELUSIONS

A delusion is defined as an incorrect belief which is inappropriate to the individual's socio-cultural background, and which is held in the face of logical argument. True delusions are fundamental errors in judgement and are as inexplicable as they are incomprehensible. They appear suddenly and are held with particular conviction. A distinction is drawn between these true or primary delusions and delusional ideas, since primary delusions are completely incomprehensible whereas delusional ideas are false but nevertheless explicable in the light of the patient's altered emotional state. For instance, in severe depression an individual can develop delusional ideas which can be explained on the grounds of his being sad and therefore believing that his life is finished, his future is hopeless etc. The delusion proper is unshakeable and incorrect and held without insight. The content of a patient's delusion reflects his past experience and is coloured by his culture pattern. Thus 100 years ago religious content in delusions was much more common than it is at the moment. Nowadays it is common for deluded patients to believe that they are being persecuted by political organizations such as the Fascists, Communists etc., or that they are being influenced by atomic explosions, radioactivity, radar, television etc. A deluded patient may also experience *ideas of reference*. This is an experience in which the patient finds that mundane happenings of even the most trifling sort have special meaning and significance for him or are directed particularly towards him. Thus a patient has found references to herself in the personal column of *The Times*, or another patient turned on a TV programme and found that all the characters were making remarks about him. *Passivity feelings* are commonly found in schizophrenia. In this the individual feels that his body or mind are under the influence of or being controlled by other people. Though paranoid delusions are not always present in a schizophrenic illness, a paranoid colouring is common.

(c) EMOTIONAL DISTURBANCE
Affective incongruity is typically found in severe schizophrenic illnesses. In this the patient's emotional display is inappropriate to his condition. In its most crude form one finds a patient laughing callously when being given some tragic news, or talking of some serious happening. In the majority of instances

we find that the emotional incongruity of schizophrenia is not so marked as the lack of emotional rapport which one can make with a schizophrenic. Many people have spoken of the pane of glass which separates one from the schizophrenic patient. It is difficult to identify with or empathize with a schizophrenic. His emotional display is limited: he is cool, detached, rather 'couldn't care less'. He is unmoved by the various things going on around him and concerned only with his own private world. Other variations of emotion are found in schizophrenia too. It is not uncommon for a schizophrenic illness to be ushered in by a state of depression or anxiety or even mild hypomanic excitement. In fact it is fair to say that any young patient i.e. adolescent patient, who presents with severe anxiety, inexplicable depression or acute hypomanic excitement must be suspected of a developing schizophrenia until it has been proved otherwise.

(d) PERCEPTUAL DISTURBANCE
The commonest perceptual disturbance of schizophrenia is the hallucination which is most commonly auditory. It is important always to enquire closely into the content and nature of the hallucinations. Patients may hear voices commenting on their actions, speaking their own thoughts aloud, uttering obscene words or phrases or telling them what to do. The voices may be familiar or unfamiliar, single or multiple. The majority of schizophrenic patients develop hallucinations at one stage or another during the illness.

(e) BEHAVIOURAL DISTURBANCE
In the development of schizophrenia one looks for alteration of the total behaviour of the individual rather than isolated phenomena. Often the relatives will describe how the individual has become more and more seclusive over a period of months, has appeared odd and made use of unfamiliar gestures, has shunned friends and familiar activities. States of ecstasy, wild excitement and impulsive behaviour also occur

in schizophrenia but probably the most common finding is a general falling off in activity. The scholar becomes less studious and the professional man less interested and able to perform his work. Periods of apparent inactivity may be interspersed with occasional bouts of rather purposeless enthusiasm for some hobby or other. Thus a schizophrenic was said to be spending much time on 'research'. When investigated this turned out to be a method of preserving butterflies' wings in some plastic substance which was somehow allied to a thesis on biochemistry. Outbursts of violence or senseless criminal acts are fortunately rare but can occur. Altered moral standards may be seen in developing schizophrenia, thus a young girl previously puritanical may become promiscuous, and it may be this concern about her sexual morals which brings her parents to consult the doctor, and the diagnosis of schizophrenia made. Any history of personality change in a young person must always raise the suspicion of schizophrenia.

Clinical Types

(a) SCHIZOPHRENIA SIMPLEX

Simple schizophrenia is characterized by a general lowering of all mental activity. The simple schizophrenic presents with poverty of activity, volition, affect and thought. This variety of schizophrenia is most commonly confused with mental subnormality. Indeed the two clinical pictures may be indistinguishable. The onset is usually slow and insidious and the prognosis in general very bad.

(b) HEBEPHRENIA

As its name implies this is seen in the younger age groups and typically the clinical picture is one of rather fatuous euphoria and hallucinosis. Here the onset tends to be insidious and the prognosis bad. Thought disorder is usually marked.

(c) CATATONIC SCHIZOPHRENIA

In catatonic schizophrenia muscle tone is altered (waxy

flexibility), strange postures are adopted. These have a symbolic meaning for the patient. Mutism and stupor occur. Repetitive words and movements can become established and fixed (stereotypy). States of wild excitement are encountered in catatonic schizophrenia. The onset is commonly acute. Other behavioural abnormalities found in catatonic schizophrenia include *automatic obedience*, in which the patient carries out every instruction given to him, *echolalia*, the repetition of the last few syllables of everything said to him and *echopraxia*, performing the same actions as the examiner.

(d) PARANOID SCHIZOPHRENIA

Characterized by the development of systems of paranoid delusions. The onset is slow and insidious. Paranoid schizophrenia is often associated with considerable preservation of the personality, so that the paranoid schizophrenic may be able to remain for a considerable time in the community and conceal his paranoid delusions. It is found in older age groups (30 and over).

General Comments on the Clinical Types

Many schizophrenic patients do not fall into any of these groups and it is questionable whether the differentiation is useful. In making the diagnosis of schizophrenia one looks for:

    (a) thought disorder,

    (b) passivity feelings,

    (c) delusions,

in particular. The history of change in personality is often the most revealing pointer.

Differential Diagnosis

The differential diagnosis of schizophrenia includes:

    (1) mania,

    (2) depression,

    (3) depression with paranoid features,

    (4) personality disorder,

    (5) hysteria.

The presence of affective disturbance of depressive type will of course always raise a suspicion of depression but it must not be forgotten that schizophrenics can be depressed.

Hysteria is often difficult to distinguish, but one looks for previous factors which would contribute to the development of an hysterical illness, such as a hysterical personality.

Treatment

No psychiatric topic is more beset with pitfalls than the treatment of schizophrenia. Since this is a poorly comprehended condition it is therefore difficult to treat adequately and impossible to treat specifically. This leads on the one hand to therapeutic nihilism and neglect of the patient and on the other to over treatment based on tenuous theory making the syndrome a perpetual testing ground. It is difficult to know which is the more dangerous of the two alternatives.

The treatment of the schizophrenic patient should consist of *a total approach to the patient*, aiming at strengthening his ties with reality and rehabilitating him. In the acute stage of the illness the patient may need to be in hospital and may have to be protected from himself since suicide commonly occurs in schizophrenia—he may need to be calmed by sedatives and tranquillizers, and his general state of health may need investigation, for co-existing physical diseases which, if found are appropriately treated.

At the present time the phenothiazine drugs, particularly *chlorpromazine* and *stelazine*, are found particularly useful to influence the mental state of the schizophrenic. These drugs not only calm but also alter perception and modify thinking. Chlorpromazine is given orally (50–200 mg t.d.s.) or by injection. Stelazine is given orally (5–15 mg t.d.s.). Intramuscular injection of fluphenazine decanoate (Modecate) 25 mgm once monthly is now established as an effective medication which many now regard as the treatment of choice. Dystonic and other extrapyramidal reactions are common but usually respond well to anti-parkinsonian drugs.

The use of E.C.T. in schizophrenia is controversial. Certainly it is of value in a schizophrenic illness of acute onset, and where affective features are present. Where it is used many authorities favour a course of twenty treatments.

Psychotherapy plays a part in the treatment of schizophrenia. It is of a supportive and reintegrative rather than analytic type. A psychotic patient cannot tolerate interpretations of his behaviour, and indeed such therapy can often be dangerously disruptive.

It is important to find useful and variable occupation for the patient. This may start with traditional occupational therapy. On the other hand there is much evidence to suggest that occupation of a constructive sort may be particularly valuable. The current interest in the reclamation of the chronic schizophrenic has shown the value of 'industrial therapy'. In industrial therapy units chronic schizophrenics perform meaningful tasks producing various objects, e.g. light industrial assembly work etc., emphasis being placed on making the situation as near to a normal work situation as possible. This encourages the patient to adopt a normal working role, and prepares him for a return to the community and the consequent return to gainful occupation.

COMMUNITY CARE OF THE SCHIZOPHRENIC PATIENT

No schizophrenic patient can be adequately treated in a social vacuum. For this reason it is important for the Doctor concerned to know as much as possible about the patient's family and home conditions. The patient who comes from a family in which there are close ties and supportive interest is liable to make better progress than the patient who is socially isolated.

Community care should therefore be more comprehensive than hospital care and is based on out-patient clinics and day hospitals. The object of community care is to avoid hospital admission wherever possible in order to avert the institutionalized apathy that the schizophrenic can so readily develop.

The Mental Health Act has invested the Local Authority

with the responsibility of organizing such services and in certain areas they are highly developed.

However there is always the danger that the patient may be overlooked if communication is poor and the General Practitioner, the hospital doctors and the Local Authority each assume that the other two are looking after him. Well organized community care involves highly developed social work by psychiatric social workers, mental welfare officers and others in collaboration with the hospital psychiatrists, general practitioners and Medical Officers of Health. Ideally the whole operation should be part of a comprehensive, community oriented mental health service.

There is much more to the follow up of patients discharged from hospital than mere attendance at an out-patient clinic now and again to receive further medication. The family of the schizophrenic patient require rather more than simple reassurance. The presence of a psychotic member in the family can be enormously disrupting and may evoke every sort of emotional response.

To ignore this and discharge a patient to an unprepared family is to invite early readmission. It is worth noting too that patients *can* be neglected at home.

Treatment of the schizophrenic patient is often difficult and unrewarding but chronicity can be avoided if emphasis is placed on strengthening the patient's ties with reality, i.e. with the community at large and facilitating his return to that community as soon as is reasonably possible and avoiding conditions of social neglect. There is much evidence to suggest that many of the features previously held to be typical of chronic schizophrenia are in fact features of social neglect.

Prognosis
Making an accurate prognosis of schizophrenia is difficult but there are a few useful pointers. The following features may be regarded as good prognostic signs
    1. Acute onset.

2. The presence of psychological or physical precipitants, e.g. child-birth, operations, etc.
3. Normal pre-morbid personality.
4. Stable social background, i.e. close social ties etc.
5. The presence of affective features.
6. Average or above average intelligence.

The following are poor prognostic features:

1. Insidious onset.
2. Persistent thought disorder.
3. Asthenic bodily habitus.
4. Presence of flattening of affect.
5. Subnormal intelligence.

REFERENCES

BOWLBY J. (1951) Maternal care and mental health. *W.H.O. Monogr.* Ser. No. 2.

FISH F. J. (1959) What is schizophrenia? *Med Progr.* (N.Y.), **242,** 97.

KALLMANN F. J. (1946) The genetic theory of schizophrenia. *Amer. J. Psychiat.* **103,** 309.

KETY S. S. (1965) Biochemical Theories of Schizophrenia. *Int. J. Psychiat.* **13,** 409–30.

KIND H. (1966) The Psychogenesis of Schizophrenia—a review of the literature. *Brit. J. Psychiat.* **112,** 333–49.

LANGFELDT G. (1956) The prognosis in schizophrenia. *Acta Psychiat. Kbh. Suppl.* 110.

LIDZ T., FLACK S. & CORNELISON (1966) *Schizophrenia in the Family.* New York: International University Press Inc.

MISHLER E. G. & SCOTCH N. A. (1965) Sociocultural Factors in the Epidemiology of Schizophrenia. *Int. J. Psychiat.* **1,** 258–93.

SMYTHIES J. (1958) Biochemical concepts of schizophrenia. *Lancet,* **ii,** 308.

WING J. K. (1961) A simple and reliable subclassification of chronic schizophrenia. *J. ment. Sci.* **107,** 862.

CHAPTER 4. ORGANIC SYNDROMES
DEMENTIA, DELIRIUM, AND
ALLIED STATES

Disturbances of cerebral function consequent on gross physical or subtle neuro-chemical damage lead to recognizable disorders which are called 'organic syndromes'. In organic syndromes the predominant impairment is of *cognitive function*. Affective symptoms, anxiety etc., are purely secondary.

Organic syndromes comprise two main groups:

(1) *Delirium and Allied Conditions*

being characterized by overactivity
clouded consciousness } acute
hallucinosis } delirium

and perplexity
clouded consciousness } subacute delirium ('confusional state')
incoherent thought

(2) *Dementia*

(a) Primary (being caused by unknown agents e.g. Pick's, Alzheimer's).

(b) Secondary (where the cause is known e.g. arteriosclerosis, tumour).

DELIRIUM AND SUBACUTE DELIRIUM

Clinical Manifestations
The most striking finding in states of delirium is the *impairment of consciousness*. In acute delirium this is severe—in its

mildest form it is found in the feelings of 'muzziness in the head' that people experience in influenza etc.

With impaired consciousness the individual's *awareness* of himself and of his surroundings is impaired. Also the level of wakefulness may be affected. The delirious child is often alarmingly bright-eyed and chatty. Wakefulness, on the other hand may be reduced, producing a drowsy appearance. With impaired awareness and recognition of the surroundings is found *poor attention* and *concentration* so that a patient when asked cannot perform simple tasks such as washing or tying his pyjama cord without getting lost halfway through. He *cannot register* the information coming in from his environment so naturally fails in tests of memory of a simple sort.

Disorientation for time and place is invariably present and severe. *Perception* is altered, either subtly or grossly. Subtle perceptual alteration is usually first noticed by the patient saying that every thing round seems clearer and sharper. Later in delirium *gross perceptual errors* occur (illusions). When this happens the patient mistakes patterns on the wall-paper for insects and animals, shadows become menacing people and bedside consultations are heard as sinister plots. Finally the patient experiences *Hallucinosis*. Visual hallucinations are common in delirium. They can take many forms. Perhaps the most common are small objects moving quickly across the visual field, e.g. in alcoholic delirium tremens patients often see small animals crawling all over the room. Hallucinations of this sort are described vividly by the patient and frequently appear clearly in his field of vision. Even their bizarre appearance is greeted without surprise, e.g. a patient recovering from chronic barbiturate intoxication saw a six inch tall manikin running around the room and hiding under the floorboards. She identified it as her husband but could not understand why no one would let her prise up the floorboards to let him out. When prevented she became homicidally violent.

Motor disturbance in delirium varies from overactivity in acute delirium to mild irritability seen in subacute delirium.

The severe overactivity can be prolonged and exhausting and represents a considerable physical hazard to the patient. The patient is restless, particularly at night, will not stay in bed, and is found wandering about the ward peering out of windows, searching and muttering to himself. He insists on leaving the ward; he must go to work; he makes a collection of his belongings, arranges and rearranges them, but such is his incoherent thinking that it all gets in a muddle and he starts all over again.

Emotional symptoms are common. States of panic and terror are usually abrupt in onset, the patient acting under the influence of his misperception of his environment. *Milder emotional symptoms* are often missed; this is unfortunate because if recognized they are useful signposts. The mildly delirious patient feels *vaguely apprehensive and uncomfortable*, and cannot say why. This may be noticed by the nurses who are surprised to find Mr X unusually uncooperative, having refused his supper.

Delusional ideas in delirium are loose and unformulated and come from the chaotic perceptions that the patient experiences. They never have the clarity and conviction of true schizophrenic delusions.

Physical Examination of the delirious patient may reveal common causes such as:

    (a) alcohol,

    (b) pneumonia,

    (c) barbiturate intoxication (chronic),

but the delirious state itself induces secondary physical changes as the patient refuses food and fluids so that he may show signs of:

    (a) dehydration,

    (b) vitamin depletion,

and further psychological disturbance, so that a vicious circle is set up.

The *diagnosis* of delirium is not difficult to make providing the examiner concentrates on establishing the state of consciousness and orientation for time and place. Impairment of consciousness and orientation do not occur in schizophrenia nor in mania.

Acute delirium is usually of short duration. Subacute delirious states can last for weeks.

DEMENTIA

Clinical Manifestations

In dementia there is *progressive and irreversible intellectual deterioration* consequent on brain damage. The damaged brain cannot absorb and store new information and this is manifest by *impairment of recent memory* which is usually the most striking finding. Patients may complain of this memory defect or it may be noticed by others and not mentioned by the patient. Often patients attempt to overcome this memory defect by keeping a notebook reminding them to do things; this is usually successful for a while but sooner or later the problem overwhelms him and he presents anxious and bewildered, fogged by a day's routine which he cannot recall. *Behaviour* shows a deterioration, *interest*, *activity* and *energy* fall off, the professional man copes less easily with his work, the housewife cannot keep up with her chores, the gas is turned on but not lit. Unusual behaviour e.g. masturbation, self-exposure, shoplifting, can appear as a release phenomenon and with its attendant legal consequences bring about the recognition of the underlying process. *The appearance* deteriorates, clothes become unkempt and stained with food. The decline is overall, leading ultimately to helpless incontinence. *Concentration* is impaired. This can be elicited easily by simple tests such as the serial subtraction of seven from one hundred. The patient is often aware of his poor ability and becomes very upset, angry, tearful and agitated when he is confronted with a task which proves too much for him. This is called the *catastrophic reaction*.

The fundamental impairments of brain function in organic brain disease are well demonstrated when this occurs. Organic brain disease produces rigidity of thinking, impairment of grasp and consequent difficulty in problem solving. Psychological tests of brain damage are designed to search for this sort of dysfunction and also to demonstrate difficulty in shifting from abstract to concrete and vice versa.

EMOTIONAL CHANGES IN DEMENTIA

There are no specific emotional disturbances. They tend to reflect in an exaggerated form the individual's previous patterns of emotional display. Lability of mood is common as control weakens and in advanced dementia one finds states of 'emotional incontinence'. Depression is common and usually ascribed to the patient's awareness of his plight. *Hysterical symptoms* may appear early in a dementing process. It is suggested that they are caused by the lower order of central nervous control and integration brought about by brain damage.

The Diagnosis of Dementia

The diagnosis of dementia is not difficult when the clinical picture is typical. However there are difficulties particularly when confronted with middle-aged patients in whom dementia may be suspected purely on the grounds of a history, say, of falling off of interest and energy for many months with some associated mood change. In such a case chronic depression may account for the whole illness, but this may not be so, and one may be left with a patient whom one has to keep under observation.

Aetiology of Dementia and Delirium

Having found signs of an organic mental state, one is next concerned with finding the underlying cause. The commonest factors causing organic mental syndromes include:

I. CEREBRAL HYPOXIA

Dementia following cerebral arteriosclerosis gradually depriving brain of oxygen.

Dementia following prolonged coma e.g. after carbon monoxide poisoning.

Delirium following cerebral haemorrhage.

Delirium associated with severe pernicious anaemia.

2. DEHYDRATION AND ELECTROLYTE IMBALANCE

Delirium due to post operative fluid loss.

Delirium in uraemia.

3. VITAMIN DEFICIENCY

Wernicke's encephalopathy.

Alcoholic delirium tremens.

4. CHRONIC INTOXICATIONS

Barbiturates.

Alcoholic—Alcoholic dementia.

5. GROSS CEREBRAL DAMAGE

Tumour.

Chronic inflammation: general paralysis.

Head injury causing post-traumatic delirium and dementia.

Investigation of Organic Syndromes

Physical examination may reveal the cause of delirium or dementia, and may reveal localizing cerebral signs. Commonly however, physical examination is negative, particularly in cases of dementia, so one employs laboratory and other investigations to clarify the picture. They include:

(1) W. R. and Kahn,

(2) skull X-ray,

(3) E.E.G.,

(4) C.S.F. Examination,

(5) air encephalogram,
(6) cerebral arteriogram.

Treatment of Organic Syndromes

GENERAL MEASURES

Delirium

The patient should be nursed in quiet surroundings with minimal interference. Calm doctors and nurses reassure the frightened delirious patient and help to maintain contact with reality however tenuous.

The evening and night time are occasions of heightened over-activity so the patient needs adequate sedation. It is wise to avoid using barbiturates and paraldehyde which may worsen confusion and produce discomfort. Phenothiazine tranquillizers can be given with safety. Diet and fluid should be kept up to the required level and symptomatic treatment with high doses of vitamins is usually given. This should take the form of intravenous parentrovite, 10 ml given 4 hourly for 24 h, then reduced to 10 ml twice daily intravenously for 24 h and then 4 ml intramuscularly daily for 5 days.

Dementia

The first thing is to find out the extent of the patient's disability so that one can provide him with an environment which is stimulating enough to prevent too rapid deterioration and not too demanding of him.

Vitamin B given by mouth is usually given, though the value of this is doubtful.

Occupational therapy and social therapy have a limited though supportive part to play by providing stimulation and preventing social deterioration.

SPECIAL MEASURES

In the treatment of delirium and dementia special measures depend on the nature of the underlying disorder if any—for example adequate anti-syphilitic treatment.

SOME SPECIAL EXAMPLES OF ORGANIC SYNDROMES

1. Conditions caused by Vitamin Deficiency

(a) KORSAKOV SYNDROME

This may be caused by thiamine deficiency, as in alcoholism, or it can be caused by tumour, cerebral trauma and general metabolic disturbance. The clinical picture includes polyneuritis with the following psychiatric symptoms:

gross impairment of recent memory
confabulation
disorientation

⎫
⎬ This type of organic picture is usually called the Dysmnesic Syndrome.
⎭

Typically the patient claims recognition of the doctor and describes in detail having met him before, when in fact he has never seen him, or will recount in detail the fancied happenings of the previous day—*confabulation*. Recent memory is so poor that though the examiner may have told the patient his name, he is unable to recollect it a minute later. The onset usually follows delerium tremens. The prognosis for complete recovery is bad.

(b) WERNICKE'S ENCEPHALOPATHY

This is caused by thiamine deficiency and is found in severe alcoholism or any state of severe malnutrition. Onset of delirium is often sudden and associated with abnormal pupils, ophthalmoplegia and nystagmus.

(c) PELLAGRA

Pellagra is caused by a mixed deficiency of tryptophan and niacin. Psychiatric abnormalities may be diverse, ranging from a neurotic to a psychotic picture, but inevitably a frank organic syndrome emerges This is usually delirium and, untreated, proceeds to dementia, coma and death.

2. Cardiovascular Disease

(a) CARDIAC FAILURE

Patients in cardiac failure are often subject to bouts of mild confusion or subacute delirium at night. This is caused by relative cerebral hypoxia and responds to further treatment of the cardiac condition.

(b) ARTERIOSCLEROTIC DEMENTIA

In cerebral arteriosclerosis the onset is earlier than in senile dementia. A typical presentation is episodic with fits, strokes, usually with complete recovery and then a picture of failing memory, concentration and personality change.

(c) THROMBOSIS OF THE INTERNAL CAROTID ARTERY

Occlusion of the internal carotid arteries can give rise to dementia usually complicated by focal cerebral signs. A typical history would include transient losses of power in one or other limbs occurring over a period of months followed by gradual alteration in memory.

3. Cerebral Syphilis
General Paralysis of the Insane (G.P.I.)

Now that syphilis is properly treated in its early stages, the full blown picture of G.P.I. is rarely seen. The first signs of G.P.I. are usually those of sudden personality change, with radical alteration of the patient's previous ethical and moral standards. This is followed by grandiose and extravagant behaviour. After this the picture settles into one of dementia with failing memory and general deterioration. The affective state is usually one of flat euphoria. Spastic paralysis, pupillary abnormalities and physical deterioration are late manifestations.

4. Syndromes following Head Injury

Dementia can follow severe head injury, as can fits which are a common sequel of head injury of whatever severity.

Traumatic Dementia usually follows extensive destruction of brain tissue. States of delirium with complete recovery can also follow severe head injury.

The term *post contusional syndrome* is usually applied to a constellation of mild chronic symptoms including headache, dizziness and general feelings of weakness and inability to concentrate. This syndrome is regarded as being constitutionally determined and released by injury. Post contusional syndromes can present difficult problems in management. In general it is advisable for patients to return to normal life and work as soon as reasonably possible since it has been found that convalescence prolonged unnecessarily delays rehabilitation and fixes neurotic symptoms.

The morale of patients is always improved by confident management, maximum reassurance and vigorous rehabilitation.

5. Other Dementias

(a) SENILE DEMENTIA

A distinction is usually drawn between senile dementia and cerebral arteriosclerosis since the latter can have its onset in the pre-senile age groups whereas by definition senile dementia comes on after the age of 65. Commonly the first manifestations of senile dementia are exaggeration of the basic changes of ageing, namely increased rigidity of thinking, greater egocentricity, lessened emotional control. These exaggerations may precede the appearance of frank evidence of dementia, while not for many years, inevitably though, memory impairment, poor concentration and impaired performance show themselves, whilst the individual's social behaviour becomes less tolerable. Neglect of the self, appearance and so on become more marked, and the individual enters a decline of all his mental powers until he ends up as an empty shell of his former self, incontinent, helpless, incapable of grasping what is going on around him.

(b) PRE-SENILE DEMENTIA

By definition pre-senile dementia can occur from any age from infancy up to the age of 65 though usually the term is used to cover the age range 45–65. The two most commonly described forms of pre-senile dementia are Alzheimer's disease and Pick's disease.

Alzheimer's disease

Here destruction of brain tissue from unknown causes affects the cortex as a whole. Abnormal affective states are commonly seen and fits may occur. The dementing process is usually fairly rapidly progressive.

Pick's disease

In this condition cerebral atrophy is mainly confined to the frontal and parietal areas, so that commonly its presentation is as a frontal lobe syndrome with impaired moral standards. This fades into a clinical picture of dementia.

(c) HUNTINGTON'S CHOREA

This is a genetically determined form of dementia. The inheritance is caused by dominant genes. The manifestations of Huntington's Chorea are choreiform movements and altered mental states leading inevitably to dementia. A wide range of psychiatric symptomatology may be seen before dementia becomes evident, although the most commonly found psychoses are paranoid in type. Suicide, alcoholism and personality disorders are common in Huntington families.

6. Syndromes Associated with Epilepsy

(a) Mood disturbance often precedes the onset of fits, or follows them.

(b) In temporal lobe epilepsy episodic mood disturbances or outbursts of rage may be caused by the epileptic discharge and be accompanied by appropriate E.E.G. changes.

(c) Personality changes are described in long standing epilepsy. The changes noted include increased religiosity, rigidity, seclusiveness and generally 'difficult' behaviour. These changes are uncommon and may well be causally related to prolonged institutionalization and the effects of excessive medication.

(d) Psychoses are found in association with epilepsy. They are schizophreniform. The current view is that these are symptomatic psychoses, i.e. psychoses having their origin in the epileptic process and not independent of it.

7. Syndromes Associated with Cerebral Tumour

The common modes of presentation of cerebral tumour are:

    (a) epilepsy,

    (b) signs of raised intracranial pressure

        e.g. headache

            papilloedema

            nausea

            vertigo

    (c) manifestations of local or generalized brain damage

        e.g. dysphasia

            apraxia

            dementia

            paresis.

However it is not uncommon for tumours to present with apparently 'pure' psychiatric symptoms. Even more misleading can be the occurrence of tumour in a patient with long standing neurotic complaints. In either instance if the doctor is not alert the diagnosis will be missed until signs of gross damage appear.

Probably about 50 per cent of patients with cerebral tumour present in this way, i.e. with psychiatric symptomatology. This places a critical diagnostic burden on anyone evaluating such symptoms, particularly in children and in patients of middle age who are most at risk for tumour development.

The following manifestations should always be enquired about most carefully, and evaluated.

1. subtle, insidious personality change
2. deterioration in appearance
3. altered ethical and moral standards
4. recent affective flattening, insouciance and apathy
5. unusual flippancy
} point to frontal lobe tumours

6. poor concentration
7. memory impairment
8. hallucinations
} point to temporal lobe tumours

9. bouts of sleepiness
} point to third ventricle tumours.

REFERENCES

BLEULER M. (1951) Psychiatry of Cerebral Diseases. *Brit. med. J.* ii, 420, 460, 463.

HARE E. H. (1959) The Origin and Spread of Dementia Paralytica. *J. ment. Sci.* **105**, 594.

KESCHNER M., BENDER M. & STRAUSS I. (1938) Mental symptoms associated with brain tumour. Study of 530 verified cases. *J. Amer. med. Ass.* **110**, 714.

SLATER E., BEARD A. W. & CLITHEROE (1963) *The Schizophrenic-like Psychoses of Epilepsy.* Brit. *J. Psychiat.* **109**, 95.

SYMONDS C. (1962) Concussion and its sequelae. *Lancet* i, 1.

WOLFF H. G. & CURRAN D. (1935) Nature of delirium and allied states. *Arch. Neurol. Psychiat.* **331**, 175.

CHAPTER 5. ABNORMAL PERSONALITY, PSYCHOPATHY AND HYSTERIA

Many people behave abnormally from their earliest years. This abnormality can show itself in antisocial acts, drug addiction, social inadequacy, undue vulnerability or in eccentricity of one sort or another. It is part of their constitution rather than an acquired illness and for this reason is ascribed to their having *abnormal personalities*.

PERSONALITY—NORMAL AND ABNORMAL

Personality is the sum of many different varying characteristics, intellectual, affective and physical, to name only a few, which gives to each person both an individuality and a resemblance to his fellows. These characteristics are present to some degree in everyone so that to speak of *normal* and *abnormal personality* is not to postulate end points separating the two categories, but rather to define an individual's personality as lying somewhere along a curve of normal distribution. In this way the abnormals are those who deviate markedly from the average and the normals are the bulk of the population. This method of considering personality has the great advantage of being *experimentally* valuable. Investigators can then go further and attempt to establish the psychological correlates of given personality characteristics. Much valuable work of this sort has already been carried out. The psychiatric approach to the study of *abnormal personalities* has in the main been a clinical one and has not been made easy to follow by the use of the term *psychopath*. In general, psychiatrists have tended

66

to call psychopaths those patients with abnormal personalities but this is not universally so. The two concepts of psychopathy and personality disorder were most succinctly united by Schneider who defined psychopaths as *those abnormal person-alities who suffer from their abnormality or cause society to suffer*. This definition is the one used in this book. It has one very important advantage, namely that it recognizes that someone can have an abnormal personality without being regarded in some way as ill or antisocial i.e. distinguishes between 'pathological' and 'non-pathological' abnormal per-sonalities. This is important because the term psychopath has come to be regarded in Anglo-American circles anyway, almost as a term of abuse.

Unfortunately the picture (in England and Wales) is made more complicated by the Mental Health Act of 1959, in which the definition of psychopathic disorder stresses irresponsible or anti-social conduct.

Psychiatrists have classified psychopaths in two main ways; first by naming groups whose personality disorder resembles a clinical syndrome, e.g. schizoid psychopath, hysterical psycho-path and secondly, by naming groups by picking out a dominant behavioural trait, e.g. inadequate psychopath, aggressive psychopath.

Variations of Abnormal Personalities

1. NON-PATHOLOGICAL

Many people of undoubted genius fall into this category. Some authorities would call them psychopaths but there seems no justification for this.

2. PATHOLOGICAL (= PSYCHOPATHS)

The abnormalities which cause symptoms include

Neuroticism
Instability
Lability of mood
Abuse of drugs

} may lead to admission to hospital.

The abnormalities which offend society include

Suicidal gestures	
Antisocial behaviour—recidivism	
Lack of foresight leading to gratification of any need	may lead to hospital,
Explosive behaviour	or more commonly
Sexual perversions	to prison.
Social inadequacy	
Inability to maintain stable interpersonal relationships	

The striking feature of so many psychopaths is their *remarkable degree of immaturity* of personality development. They react to the whim of the moment in much the same way as does a small child who has tantrums if his wishes are not gratified immediately. The same sort of thing leads them into crimes which can have disastrous consequences.

Treatment

There is no treatment which can transform someone's personality, on the other hand prolonged psychotherapy can be helpful to the intelligent psychopath—it is a way of focusing on his problems whilst he forms a relationship with the therapist

Social rehabilitation of the antisocial psychopath is attempted by group therapy in special communities (therapeutic community). In these, the traditional hierarchical hospital structure is done away with since psychopaths do not do well in such a situation. Instead the approach to the patient acknowledges the importance of social forces and of the community as a whole in influencing behaviour. The unit is run on democratic rather than autocratic lines and the whole community of patients and staff share the responsibility for determining the behaviours that they can tolerate (Rapaport 1960). There is growing evidence to show that psychopaths do well in such units.

MEDICATION

(a) Tranquillizers and sedatives may be used in helping psychopaths through crises but there is no justification for routine long-term medication except in the case of aggressive psychopaths who can be kept calm with phenothiazines.

(b) Antidepressive drugs may be used when sustained depression is encountered.

HYSTERIA

The word hysteria is used in at least four ways.

(1) To describe a variety of abnormal personality: *Hysterical personality*.

(2) To describe certain disorders, *hysterical disorders (conversion hysteria)*, in which there is loss of function without organic damage. These disorders are induced by stress and the patient is unconscious of the mechanism.

(3) To describe unconscious exaggeration of organic disease, so called '*hysterical overlay*' or 'hysterical exaggeration'.

(4) To describe states of mind in which an individual becomes 'out of control', 'beside herself'. This is a lay use of the term, but used surprisingly frequently by doctors.

1. Hysterical Personality

The term 'hysterical personality' is used to describe a particular type of individual who is himself the more likely to develop hysterical symptoms. Such individuals show the following traits:

(a) Affective immaturity often allied to an appearance of physical immaturity.

(b) Egocentricity allied to a remarkable capacity for self deception.

(c) Histrionic behaviour. To the hysteric the world is either hell or heaven. Extremes of feeling easily aroused and

F

as easily dissipated are commonplace. This is reflected in their appearance in striking fashion. At one moment the patient is an ashen faced weeping wreck threatening suicide, disrupting the whole atmosphere of the ward—hours later or less, she is the most vivacious and sought after partner at the hospital dance.

(d) Inability to tolerate or maintain inter-personal relationships of any depth.

Of course the hysteric possesses these traits to an excessive degree—they are common enough in normal people. Under certain circumstances the hysterical personality can be an asset e.g. in the theatre.

2. Hysterical Disorders (conversion hysteria)

In hysterical disorders there is loss of function without organic damage. This arises as a result of stress usually in a susceptible person but can occur in otherwise normal individuals in face of overwhelming stress (e.g. disasters, wartime etc.).

The lost function protects the patient from further harm. 'Is the illness simulated?' it may be asked. The answer is 'Yes, but the patient is wholly or partly unaware of this'.

Hysterical disorders may be of a wide variety. Most commonly they affect higher functions and the central nervous system producing amnesia, paralysis, sensory loss etc. Hysteria can also produce pseudo dementia in which the patient develops an apparent psychotic state. The signs of 'psychosis' confirm to the layman's idea of madness, e.g. when asked how many legs has a cow a patient might answer 'five'. Pains can be hysterical in origin. When this is so it is a common error to suppose that the patient is therefore not experiencing discomfort but is feigning. As so little is known about the mechanism of pain there seems no justification for this belief. It is wiser to acknowledge that the patient is in pain and try and discover the cause. Pain is pain whether hysterical or not, and the label hysterical should not be allowed to cause patients to be subjected to the sort of hostile treatment that they may provoke by their admittedly often demanding and rather ruthless behaviour.

Aetiology of Hysteria

1. The role of the hysterical personality has been mentioned. There is strong evidence to support the belief that genetic factors are important in this.

2. It is likely too that upbringing can reinforce already dominant hysterical traits. The doting parent who accedes to every whim of an unstable egocentric child is probably doing this unwittingly.

3. *Brain damage, mental subnormality and chronic psychosis* all predispose to hysteria by lowering higher control and integration.

4. Hysterical disorders are danger signals. The undiagnosed depressive or the incipient schizophrene who finds his inner life mysteriously disrupted—both may develop hysterical symptoms as an unconscious call for help.

5. The manifestations of hysteria conform to:

   (a) the patient's notion of illness, thus sensory loss is of 'glove' or 'stocking' distribution.

   (b) ideas of disease implanted in the patient's mind by others either by suggestion or example. Doctors can suggest the former and other patients the latter by their own symptoms.

6. The psychodynamic explanation of hysterical disorder is that the failure in function always arises as a result of unconscious conflict or buried psychic trauma which threaten the individual's integrity to such an extent that he responds by switching off a function thus making it unnecessary to continue in the stressful situation as he is now ill and can opt out of the situation demanding his attention. This switching off is referred to as dissociation.

Diagnosis of Hysteria

Since hysteria can mimic so many other illnesses the differential diagnosis is limitless. The diagnosis should be made on positive and not negative grounds; it is not good enough to investigate a patient's complaints and, having found no abnormality, fall back on hysteria as a convenient dumping ground.

One must have adequate reasons for making the diagnosis so that one can look at the patient's history and life situation and see with certainty that a hysterical disorder is the inevitable outcome of all that has gone before.

Hysteria is a diagnosis that is often made lightly by the inexperienced, purely on the basis of a few negative results.

Treatment of Hysteria

(a) HYSTERICAL PERSONALITY DISORDER

Such patients usually make brief dramatic appearances in hospital following suicidal gestures, marital strife or any acute stress that is too much for their level of tolerance. Mood disturbances may be prominent but rarely sustained.

Tranquillizing drugs may be needed to calm the patient in a period of acute crisis. The object should be to make the period of hospital stay as short as possible to tide the patient over the crisis.

After this, treatment either consists of:

(1) Simple supportive therapy,

(2) Prolonged psychotherapy aimed at helping the patient towards insight and a higher level of emotional maturity.

(b) HYSTERICAL DISORDER (CONVERSION HYSTERIA)

General

It is important to treat the patient actively i.e. to do everything possible that will help to convince him that total function will return. At the same time one has to avoid focusing too much on the symptom and reinforcing it in the patient's mind.

This can be done fairly easily as long as doctors and nurses approach the patient as a team and with full knowledge of each other's roles. Difference of opinion and uncertainty feed hysteria. The patient, sensing differing attitudes, questions different people, gets different answers and his symptoms intensify and proliferate.

Abreaction

Freud used this term to describe the re-living of emotionally charged experiences said to have caused hysterical breakdown. Abreaction has a place in the treatment of hysteria but is most successful in the acute disorder, i.e. immediately following some traumatic experience.

Abreaction is encouraged in a state of altered consciousness —usually brought about by giving intravenous sodium amytal (250 mg–500 mg). In theory the patient regains the lost function once he has ventilated the pent-up feeling that surrounds the traumatic scene.

Psychotherapy

The alternatives are:

(a) supportive therapy,

(b) commencing exploratory psychotherapy with the object of helping the patient to understand the nature of his illness and how it relates to his life situation. This means embarking on fairly prolonged psychotherapy.

REFERENCES

CURRAN D. & MALLINSON P. (1944) Psychopathic personality. *J. ment. Sci.* 90, 266.

HENDERSON D. K. (1939) *Psychopathic States.* Norton, New York.

LJUNDBERG (1957) Hysteria, a genetic and prognostic survey. *Acta Psychiat. et Neurol. Scand. suppl.* 112, 22.

SCOTT P. D. (1960) The treatment of psychopaths. *Brit. med. J.* i, 1641.

SCHNEIDER K. (1958) *Psychopathic personalities*. Cassell, London.

SLATER E. (1965) Diagnosis of Hysteria. *Brit. med. J.* i, 1395–1399.

CHAPTER 6. OBSESSIONAL ILLNESS

Obsessions and compulsions are similar though not identical psychological manifestations. Their similarity lies in the fact that they are both experienced against an inner feeling of resistance. Obsessions are contents of consciousness i.e. ideas or thoughts which the patient has and which he tries to push away. Sometimes they develop into acts, utterances or rituals, and become repetitive, in which case they are called compulsions. In practice they are described collectively by the term obsessive compulsive phenomena.

Aetiology

1. NORMAL DEVELOPMENT
Everyone has experienced the 'tune that keeps running through the head', or the rituals practised in childhood e.g. walking on paving stones avoiding the lines. These are part of normal life and development and resemble obsessive compulsive phenomena. Children often use these rituals in a magical way to defend themselves from fancied harm. It has been suggested that rituals are used in a similar way in obsessional illness.

2. PERSONALITY TYPE
Some people are from their early years over meticulous and unduly scrupulous. They show excessive concern for order and tidiness in dress and in their surroundings. Their talk is precise, even pedantic, while their outlook is excessively moral and rigid. They tend to be indecisive, vacillatory and hypochondriacal. Their indecisiveness makes them good subordinates but poor leaders. They lack imagination or creative ability, and humour, when present, is of an arid donnish sort. These

sort of traits constitute the *obsessional personality*. If such people become psychologically ill, they develop obsessional symptoms. When such individuals develop say a depressive state, their illness tends to be very much coloured by their personality so that they often present with an interminable kind of pedantic hypochondriacal talk which may mask the depressive mood change which becomes more apparent as the interview proceeds.

3. RELATION TO BRAIN DAMAGE

(a) Obsessional symptoms are definitely associated with the personality changes following encephalitis lethargica.

(b) The brain damaged patient often develops obsessional tidiness, 'organic orderliness'. This can be seen as the way in which a progressively handicapped individual attempts to impose order on an environment that is becoming too much for him.

Manifestations of Obsessional Illness

Obsessional symptoms tend to focus on daily activities such as eating, dressing, washing and defaecation—a patient complained that she was unable to eat as she spent hours removing solid particles from food matter—another patient never finished her house work as she felt obliged to repeat the washing-up time and time again—a patient could not get to work on time as he was delayed by elaborate rituals surrounding his morning defaecation.

Usually the patient seeks medical advice because the symptom has *got out of hand*. It has usually been present for some time but recently become troublesome.

Mood change of a depressive sort is a common association, obsessions get worse with depression and vice versa, so a vicious circle is set up.

Anguish, anxiety and tension are frequent accompaniments. The obsessional's tendency to self-criticism is unduly exaggerated. He describes the symptoms of his illness in strongly self-condemnatory terms, apparently quite failing to see it all as illness at all, when any of his friends etc., quite easily recognize that he is unwell.

Diagnosis

The pure obsessional illness is often hard to distinguish from a depressive illness with obsessional features since depression usually accompanies the former. The history, however, should be helpful.

Schizophrenia may present as an obsessional illness, or obsessional features may complicate it. This can present a tricky diagnostic problem. Obsessions associated with schizophrenia tend to be rather bizarre.

Treatment

1. PSYCHOTHERAPY

Analytic psychotherapy of obsessional illness aims at discovering the symbolic meaning of the phenomena, for the psychoanalytic view of obsessional illness is that it results from overactivity of the superego which defends the ego against overwhelming anxiety by magical rituals. In practice obsessionals do not respond particularly well to psychotherapy, their pedantry and excessive concern with detail cause them to become enmeshed in the therapeutic process and brought to a halt.

Supportive therapy however can help the patient to ventilate pent up feelings about his rituals and afford him some relief of anxiety and tension.

2. MEDICATION

(a) Tranquillizers can be useful in reducing anxiety. The most useful is librium which should be administered to the limit of tolerance.

(b) Antidepressive drugs should always be tried whenever there is any evidence of depression.

3. PHYSICAL TREATMENT

(a) E.C.T. is useful in the presence of depression.

(b) Leucotomy is used in the treatment of chronic severe obsessional disorder accompanied by persistent tension and misery.

Natural History and Prognosis

Obsessional illnesses show phases of remission and exacerbation (Pollitt 1960) so that the long-term outlook is not so gloomy as is sometimes feared. Nevertheless the illness can be crippling. It is useful to use social criteria in assessing the degree of handicap e.g. one should try and find out how long per day the patient spends on his rituals; do they prevent him from working or is he late for work etc.?

The presence of depression of any degree makes the outlook better.

REFERENCES

GRIMSHAW L. (1965) The Outcome of Obsessional disorder; a follow up study of 100 cases. *Brit. J. Psychiat.* **111**, 1051–1056.

KRINGLEN E. (1965) Obsessional neurotics—a long term follow up. *Brit. J. Psychiat.* **111**, 709–22.

LEWIS A. J. (1935) Problems of obsessional illness. *Proc. roy. Soc. Med.* **29**, 325.

POLLITT J. (1960) Natural history studies in mental illness. *J. ment. Sci.* **106**, 442.

CHAPTER 7. ALCOHOLISM AND DRUG DEPENDENCE

ACUTE ALCOHOLISM

This is a condition which is commonly encountered in medical practice. Acute alcoholic intoxication is a familiar sight and is adequately described in medical textbooks. It can be a fatal condition particularly when it is misdiagnosed in the presence of closed or open head injury.

CHRONIC ALCOHOLISM AND ALCOHOL ADDICTION

Chronic alcoholism is a state in which a patient becomes dependent on alcohol to such a degree that it interferes with his physical and psychological health and impairs his professional ability and social relations. It includes alcoholic addiction which is really only an exaggeration of it, the only difference being that the addict drinks increasing quantities and is more likely to develop physical and psychological symptoms on withdrawal from alcohol. Also he craves it.

It is important to emphasize that there is a difference between addiction and chronic alcoholism. All addicts are alcoholics but not all alcoholics are addicts. Addiction is easily diagnosed. Chronic alcoholism is not.

Incidence
The incidence of chronic alcoholism is hard to estimate. A conservative estimate puts the figure at 500,000 in the United Kingdom.

The importance of the recognition of chronic alcoholism lies in the fact that it is a destructive process. It destroys health, personal relationships, professional life and prospects, and unchecked, leads to disaster.

Aetiology

Not precisely known though family studies of alcoholics show a high loading of psychosis and personality disorder. The simplest view of aetiology acknowledges no specific agent but would take into consideration first of all the *symptomatic alcoholic*, i.e. an individual who resorts to alcohol in the course of an illness such as depression or schizophrenia. Such patients account for less than 10 per cent of chronic alcoholics.

Alcoholism may be a feature of personality disorder admittedly but the bulk of alcoholics do not fall into a homogeneous group no matter how they are studied. Commonly the alcoholic becomes such from a combination of factors—he may drink to relieve neurotic anxiety, or to escape from his difficult life situation. Certain occupations present a significant risk of alcoholism e.g. barmen, commercial travellers.

Manifestations

INTRODUCTION

There is a pattern in the history of chronic alcoholism which at least can aid in the diagnosis. The following are found to be signs that drinking is getting out of control:

> gulping,
> taking extra drinks before parties,
> drinking on the way home,
> drinking during the day,
> lying about one's consumption of alcohol,
> avoiding the topic of alcohol in conversation,
> concealing alcohol on the person,
> carrying drink to work,
> taking 'liveners' on rising,
> amnesic gaps.

The incipient alcoholic passes through a stage of habitual excessive drinking bouts till he is drinking all the time.

The full blown clinical picture may be easily recognized by the familiar picture of the red-faced, obese, probably bronchitic, toper, moving from saloon bar joviality to maudlin tears or uncontrolled anger with easy rapidity.

Physical complications of chronic alcoholism include:
nausea,
gastritis,
diarrhoea,
hepatic cirrhosis, liver failure, portal systemic encephalopathy,
piles,
pancreatitis,
bronchitis,
pulmonary tuberculosis,
peripheral neuritis.

PSYCHOLOGICAL MANIFESTATIONS
Apart from the psychological changes already described there are certain complicating syndromes, namely:

Alcoholic Hallucinosis
A condition characterized by auditory hallucinations of long standing followed by the development of paranoid delusions. It is controversial whether this is a syndrome in its own right or merely the incidence of schizophrenia in an alcoholic.

Typically the onset is insidious and remits if the patient abstains from alcohol.

Delirium Tremens
As the name implies this a state of restlessness and impaired consciousness associated with tremors. The onset usually follows alcoholic withdrawal and may be heralded by a twenty-four hour prodromal period in which apprehension is

prominent, also misinterpretation of the environment, mild disorientation and fits.

The florid clinical picture reveals an excited hallucinated (visually and aurally) patient, misinterpreting his environment in paranoid fashion and in an affective state of terror.

He is usually restless and febrile.

Treatment. Nursing in a darkened room, the provision of plenty of fluid, vitamin saturation and the use of phenothiazine tranquillizers will restore to normal contact with reality in under 36 hours.

Korsakov's Syndrome
A syndrome of gross impairment of recent memory with a tendency to confabulate answers. This syndrome was originally described in alcoholics but can also be caused by arteriosclerosis etc.

Alcoholic Dementia
There is nothing particular about the condition apart from the aetiology. An extremely insidious onset is the rule.

Treatment and Prevention of Alcoholism
The first step in treatment is withdrawal from alcohol. This can only be achieved in hospital and the successful treatment of alcoholism depends on this initial step followed by abstention. Withdrawal is not difficult to manage; it requires a degree of cooperation which reflects the patient's intention to get rid of the habit. And of course, the patient is under no compulsion to do this.

There is no point in prolonging the agony by giving diminishing quantities of alcohol, it is better to stop completely and be prepared to treat any complications which follow e.g. fits or delirium tremens.

Sedatives such as barbiturates are best avoided in the withdrawal period; most workers prefer to use phenothiazine tranquillizers (Chlorpromazine, Promazine) to allay restlessness, combined with *vitamin saturation* and plenty of fluid and nourishment. Another valuable medication in alcohol withdrawal is chlormethiazole (Hemineverin). This is a sedative and anticonvulsant that many regard as the ideal medication. It may be given intravenously, e.g. in the case of associated severe illness.

Once the withdrawal period is over one is faced with the problem of encouraging abstention from alcohol for the rest of the patient's life.

There are several ways of approaching this problem; none is complete in itself.

First, by medication, disulfiram (antabuse) provides a chemical defence against alcohol for the patient so that if he takes a drink when on regular antabuse medication, he gets an unpleasant reaction in which he feels unwell, flushes and collapses. The success of this treatment depends on the degree of cooperation that the patient is willing to offer.

The main forms of help offered to the alcoholic are psychotherapeutic and social.

Individual psychotherapy probably has little to offer the alcoholic but the available evidence suggests that group psychotherapy in specialized units has, by helping the alcoholic to see his difficulties in perspective, and to come to terms with the problems that drink provides for him, and the problems created for him by abstention. Not least it may show him the problems that force him to drink. A telling comment on this was made by a patient who said 'It's all very well asking me to give up drink but what are you going to put in its place?'

Alcoholics Anonymous (A.A.) plays a great part in the treatment of the alcoholic and its help should be offered to all. It is an organization of alcoholics devoted to helping each other to abstain from drink and has the great merit of being founded on common sense principles of a semi-religious sort.

The symptomatic alcoholic is treated by treating first of all the underlying condition.

Prognosis
Prognosis is not precise but a few general comments can be
made. The sounder the individual's personality the better the
prognosis. The shorter the duration of alcoholism the better.
Occupations leading to alcoholism made the prognosis worse
(barmen etc.).

DRUG DEPENDENCE

Drug dependence has become a problem causing increased
medical and social concern. This was revealed by the increased
incidence of self-injection with heroin and similar drugs by
younger people within recent years. As might be expected
when this phenomenon was examined it then became apparent
that the problems of drug misuse amongst younger people were
perhaps more extensive than had been realized. The common
drugs of dependence may be considered under three headings,
stimulant, sedative and hallucinogenic drugs.

Drugs with a predominantly sedative-type action
These fall into two groups. First of all there are the sedative
analgesics—in other words the opiate and opioid drugs of
which the most highly prized by the user would be heroin and
morphine. These are usually taken intravenously and a full
blown syndrome of dependence is characterized by the presence
of physical and psychological dependence, the former being
manifest by physical withdrawal symptoms if the drug is dis-
continued and the latter by a good deal of personal involve-
ment with drug use and often by the alteration in a person's
way of life so that he becomes very closely involved with a life
style in which drug usage is the main activity. This can end up
with a state of social neglect where the user spends all his time
and money getting hold of drugs and neglecting himself.
There are no specific signs of dependence itself though injection marks on the arms and legs are common. The opiate

abstinence syndrome includes restlessness, irritability, abdominal cramps, nausea, rhinitis and diarrhoea. Withdrawal from heroin should be carried out gradually and it is customary to use this period to improve the patient's physical state with vitamins, fluids, food and tranquillizers. Heroin is reduced gradually and replaced by methadone by mouth. This drug has the effect of a longer duration of action and is a valuable way of treating withdrawal symptoms. Detoxification is of course only the first stage and is followed by the most difficult aspects of treatment, namely, the encouragement of abstention. In general encouraging patients towards abstention can be said to rest on two principles, the first of which is to try and find an alternative satisfaction in the patient's life to the use of drugs and this can be done by social means where one tries to provide the patient with a different life altogether. Notable examples of this sort of manoeuvre would be the Phoenix Houses, which started in America, where patients commit themselves to a drug-free life and work out their problems in vigorous open encounter sessions. Though the relapse rate is high in opiate dependence it is unwise to take too pessimistic a view since a great deal can be done to improve the physical and psychological status of all drug users. The second approach is to try and substitute another drug for the heroin and current practice favours the use of Methadone in this respect.

Sedative Drugs

These for the most part would include barbiturates and a large number of non-barbiturate sedatives. The former are often prescribed in a rather unwise fashion, producing chronic barbiturate intoxication and dependence which may arise far more frequently than may be suspected. In chronic barbiturate intoxication are found slurred speech, nystagmus and ataxia with various states of confusion. Withdrawal from barbiturates often produces fits and the withdrawal period should be treated by gradual detoxification, using pentobarbitone in divided doses reducing by 100 mgs daily.

G

Stimulant Drugs

The commonest in use are those of the amphetamine type including dexedrine, drinamyl, amphetamine and preludin. These drugs, taken by people of normal and abnormal personality for their stimulant effect produce a short-lived feeling of well-being followed by gloom inducing the taker to consume larger quantities of the drug so that up to 2 g per 24 h may be consumed.

States of *restlessness and irritability* with outbursts of anger are common but probably the most serious manifestation is *amphetamine psychosis* (Connell 1954). This is a syndrome of restlessness, elation, paranoid ideas and hallucinosis i.e. a schizophreniform psychosis which clears up after withdrawal.

The treatment of amphetamine dependence is made more difficult by its prevalence amongst psychopaths and also by its unwise prescription. It should be emphasized that the clear indications for the uses of amphetamines are really only three: (1) narcolepsy, (2) in oversedated epileptic patients, and (3) in the treatment of hyperkinetic children.

Hallucinogenic drugs

Hallucinogenic drugs have been more widely misused in recent years since the early 1960's. The most commonly misused drug is lysergic acid (LSD) and although it does not produce any physical dependence it certainly can cause states of psychological dependence where the individual overvalues its supposed effects on his mental state. Unhappily LSD is associated with adverse reactions and in general these tend to fall into three types; first of all states of acute psychotic excitement, secondly chronic depressive states and thirdly states of panic and terror, often followed by persistent symptoms of depersonalization. Fortunately the majority of LSD adverse reactions appear to subside relatively spontaneously though ideally such patients should receive psychiatric supervision and admission where necessary.

Aetiology of Drug Dependence

(a) People rarely become dependent on drugs by accident, for example severe therapeutic dependence remains uncommon. It should be remembered that dependency producing drugs are in general 'mind altering'—i.e. they may affect feeling, perception, thinking and behaviour. Also the user will have heard about the supposed effects and wants to try them out. This means that dependence may follow a repeated pleasant drug induced effect or follow the use of a drug which abolishes some unpleasant subjective symptoms and these include not only the abolition of withdrawal symptoms, but in some cases neurotic anxiety etc., so that the drug becomes a form of self-medication.

(b) The terms 'hard' and 'soft' drugs are misleading. A more useful distinction may however be drawn between those who inject themselves with drugs and those who swallow them. The former group are more likely to develop severe varieties of dependence and fairly quickly at that, also they have an associated morbidity and mortality from the effects of unsterile self-injection.

(c) Society is presently most concerned about drug use amongst young males for hedonic reasons. But these patients, though they present urgent social problems should not deflect interest in the wider problems of 'hidden' dependency on sedatives, hypnotics and tranquillisers.

(d) A useful way of regarding drug dependence is to realise that it often involves 'drug using behaviour' i.e. a life style, rather than mere pharmacological dependence. At present youthful drug dependence is notable for subcultural drug use, and attitudes and a view of the world that may go with it. Multiple drug use is becoming more common.

(e) Drug dependence, though it may ostensibly be related to such ephemera as 'curiosity', 'a new experience' etc. is in severe cases an outgrowth of longstanding personality disorder—often of psychopathic dimensions, but this *does not account for all cases*. Some may use drugs to relieve anxiety and depression or as a barrier between themselves and a world which they find unacceptable. While for the delinquency oriented youngster drugs may provide an easy source of illicit gratification.

(f) Regarding the aetiology of drug dependence, facts are hard to come by. Speculation is universal.

REFERENCES

BEWLEY T. H. (1965) Heroin Addiction in the U.K. (1954–1964). *Brit. med. J.* ii, 1284–6.

BEWLEY T. H. (1965) Heroin and Cocaine Addiction. *Lancet*, i, 808–10.

CONNELL P. H. (1958) Amphetamine psychosis. London. Chapman & Hall.

JELLINEK E. M. (1960) Alcoholism, a genus and some of its species. *Canad. Med. Ass. J.* 83, 1341.

KESSEL N. & GROSSMAN G. (1961) Suicide in alcoholics. *Brit. med. J.* ii, 1671.

W.H.O. Expert Committee on Mental Health (1955) *Alcohol and Alcoholism*. Tech Rep. W.H.O. No. 94.

WILLIS J. H. (1969) *Drug Dependence*. London. Faber.

CHAPTER 8. SUBNORMALITY

Introduction

Individuals who are found to have 'arrested or incomplete' mental development *from birth* are usually described as being *mentally subnormal*. Their fundamental defect is one of intelligence. However, they usually have other degrees of psychological and social handicap which may be accompanied by physical disabilities often of considerable severity. It is therefore important to be aware of the multiplicity of problems and difficulties that may beset the subnormal patient. Failure to recognize this from the outset can result in the subnormal patient not receiving the detailed attention, advice and treatment which he and his relatives invariably require. It is this increased awareness of the complexity of the problems of subnormality which has led to a much more hopeful attitude in treatment.

INTELLIGENCE

An acceptable working definition of intelligence is that it is a general ability which enables the individual to learn from experience, form judgements, handle concepts and modify behaviour. Intelligence is not regarded as a fixed unvarying entity but as something modifiable by environment, i.e. by education and favourable upbringing. Also it is apparent that the extent to which people utilize their intelligence is influenced by their level of motivation, emotional stability and maturity.

Experimental evidence shows too that intelligence is *multifactorial* that is to say a general level of ability subsumes certain special abilities all of which correlate highly with each other.

Measurement of Intelligence

Tests have been devised which are tests of ability. They are *standardized* for *large populations* and are *reliable* (i.e. when repeated on the same person give the same answer) and *valid* (i.e. measure what they are meant to measure).

INTELLIGENCE QUOTIENT (I.Q.)

This is a numerical way of expressing the level of intelligence. Originally the I.Q. was estimated by the calculation.

$$\frac{\text{Mental Age}}{\text{Chronological Age}} \times 100$$

Since the first attempts to measure intelligence (Binet) took as their unit of measurement the *mental age* i.e. the average level of ability that could be predicted for given age groups. It will be realized therefore that to a large extent the I.Q. may be an unreliable figure.

At the present time the *measurement of intelligence* is based on estimations of the deviations from the mean scores obtained by individuals in the same age groups as the person being tested. Tests are *standardized* by being given to a representative sample of a population, stratified by age. For any given age group, the mean score obtained is given an arbitrary value of 100 (i.e. the average I.Q. is assumed to be 100), and the standard deviation of I.Q. levels is set at 15 points.

In this way, when the distribution of I.Q.'s is plotted it is found that, like the distribution of stature, the curve approximates to the so called 'normal' distribution. That is to say the majority of cases cluster around the mean, and cases which differ markedly from the mean are comparatively rare.

Using a standardized intelligence test, approximately one half of the population will score between 90 and 110 points and about two-thirds between 85 and 115 points. Ninety-five per cent of the population will have I.Q.'s between 70 and 130 (i.e. two standard deviations either side of the mean).

On the whole lower intelligence is rather more common than high intelligence or put in statistical terms the curve is negatively skewed. This suggests that while the majority of individuals of low intelligence are normal variants, there are a certain proportion whose intellectual defect arises as a result of disease, injury or metabolic disturbance.

However, it has to be recognized that since the I.Q. is to a certain extent an arbitrary score, it is difficult to be precise about the true distribution of intelligence. With this in mind it can be seen that the intelligence quotient, particularly when the figure is a low one, can be very misleading without a total appreciation of the psychological and social characteristics of the individual under consideration.

The estimation of subnormality of intelligence is therefore made by measuring the I.Q. At present the cut off points are that subnormality of intelligence is said to exist if the I.Q. is below 70 points and severe subnormality if the I.Q. is below 50 points.

However, the position is made somewhat more difficult by the Mental Health Act which defines both subnormality and severe subnormality without reference to psychometry.

In the Mental Health Act the subnormal are defined as persons suffering from a 'state of arrested or incomplete development of mind (not amounting to severe subnormality) which includes subnormality of intelligence and is of a nature or degree which requires or is susceptible to medical treatment or other special care or training of the patient' This attempt at categorization would include those patients formerly described as 'feeble minded'.

The severely subnormal are defined as persons suffering from a 'state of arrested or incomplete development of mind which includes subnormality of intelligence and is of such a nature or degree that the patient is incapable of living an independent life or of guarding himself against serious exploitation, or will be so incapable when of an age to do so'. This description includes patients who would formerly have been described as 'idiots' or 'imbeciles', in addition to the lower grades of those patients formerly termed 'feeble minded'.

SUBNORMALITY

General Considerations

Many subnormal patients are otherwise 'normal' people whose intelligence is in the extreme low ranges of the frequency distribution curve. Others, however, are individuals of potentially higher intelligence who have experienced brain damage. The latter would include those affected by rubella in the first three months of foetal life or head injury or encephalitis in infancy. Others include individuals with genetically determined metabolic disorders which inhibit normal brain development and function. On the other hand there are individuals who are subnormal by reason of intellectual, emotional or social deprivation in early life. A child reared in a brutalizing atmosphere is likely to score many points lower on I.Q. tests than another child of equal ability coming from a more favourable home. It should be remembered too that limited intelligence does not mean that the patient lacks commonsense. Clinical experience of interviewing the subnormal patient constantly reaffirms this fact.

In addition to all this subnormal patients are commonly weighed down by other handicaps such as poor vision or deafness which prevent them from making the most effective use of their available intelligence. The presence of disturbances such as epilepsy or birth induced cerebral palsy are not uncommon and of course can provide further handicap. Subnormal patients are often, but not always, emotionally as well as intellectually immature. Also the severely subnormal often has a dysplastic physique with a small brain and head and may display hyperkinetic syndromes in childhood.

The Management of the Subnormal Patient

CHILDREN

Subnormal children develop better both from the point of view of their intelligence and also as far as social ability goes providing they spend their childhood in the family setting. Parents will accept the subnormal child as long as they are given sensible explanation and advice. It is particularly important to recognize that the parents may feel incompetent, helpless, resentful, frustrated, in fact a wide variety of conflicting emotions when confronted with the realization that the child is handicapped in this way. It is therefore particularly important that this sort of advice and support should be readily available when the abnormality is first recognized or when slow development is first suspected by either parent, doctor or health visitor. Full paediatric assessment is essential so that treatable metabolic disorders may be discovered. In addition sensory handicaps such as blindness or deafness should be recognized. And the problems of speech disorder, dyslexia and epilepsy may be recognized.

EDUCATIONAL REQUIREMENTS

The majority of children with I.Q.'s over 55 are 'educable' in that they will be able to learn the rudiments of reading and writing and they will be able to attend schools run by their Education Authority. Those who are most backward in this group are classified as *educationally subnormal* and sent to special schools.

Children with I.Q.'s below 50 are excluded from school though the majority can benefit from education given in *day training centres*, run by the local authority. The majority of E.S.N. school leavers manage to function as ordinary if somewhat limited people when they leave school and only a minority ever come to the notice of the local Mental Health Authority. Most of them settle down in time, find work, and present no great problem. A few may require institutional care which in every case should be on a voluntary basis to either residential home or hospital.

Severely subnormal children often make extremely good progress at day training centres and many achieve adult life able to work in sheltered surroundings. The most severely handicapped, and it must be emphasized that these are a minority, require to be fed and dressed and have pretty long-term care. After childhood, long stay hospital care will be necessary.

There are two definite indications for long-term care of the subnormal or the severely subnormal individual away from home. They are:

1. Possibility of obtaining better education or treatment of a degree sufficient to outweigh the disadvantages of being away from home, 2. Where the patient's family is suffering from his presence in the home.

Thus it emerges that the criteria for admission to long stay hospitals for the mentally subnormal are largely social.

While it is true that a proportion of severely subnormal patients may require prolonged hospital care, it is increasingly realized that the basic needs of these patients are the same as those of their more generously endowed fellows, i.e. they need affection, warmth, social acceptance, education and employment. Given the right sort of environment any subnormal patient can find a more congenial and productive life in the community than he can in an institution. With this in mind day centres, occupational training centres and the like, are excellent examples of the sort of community oriented projects that foster enlightened care of such patients.

Subnormal patients can and do learn tasks that were previously supposed to be beyond their level of ability, providing that the teaching is carried out in a sensible patient way. Tasks may need to be broken down in various ways and the patient may need to learn via one sensory channel rather than by being given a variety of instructions all at the same time. Above all he needs a climate where failure is not penalized and where emotional outbursts are accepted with sympathy and understanding.

The family of the subnormal child need help if they are to keep him at home or if he has to go into hospital. This help includes not only practical advice but also psychological support and understanding of the emotional problems posed by his very being. Guilt, resentment, anxiety, over protection and denial are all common reactions and merit sensible acceptance and free discussion between doctor and parents. This is one area where such communication can be of inestimable value.

SPECIAL SYNDROMES ASSOCIATED WITH SUBNORMALITY

1. Down's Syndrome (Mongolism)

Langdon-Down (1887) first described this syndrome and likened the appearance of the affected child to that of a member of the mongol race. This resemblance is based on incorrect assumptions about the appearance of the race and has given rise to discontent with the use of the term.

The incidence of the condition is approximately 1 in 650 births. Affected individuals show a characteristic appearance of which the main features are:

(a) broad nose,
(b) flattened head,
(c) enlarged tongue,
(d) oblique eyelids,
(e) short fingers.

There is an increased incidence of congenital heart lesions amongst sufferers and this contributes to their diminished life expectation.

AETIOLOGY
(a) Mongolism occupies a special place in the history of medicine since it was the first syndrome ever shown to be due

to a chromosomal abnormality. In 1959 Lejeune, Gauthier & Turpin demonstrated the presence of an extra chromosome—hence the name *Trisomy 21*. (This indicates the position of the extra chromosome.) This discovery opened up a vast field of interest in the relationships of chromosomal abnormalities to various conditions.

(b) Increased maternal age bears a definite relationship to the condition.

2. Phenyl Pyruvic Oligophrenia

This is a syndrome associated with an inborn metabolic error. Affected individuals are subnormal and have fair hair and skin and blue eyes. There is a significant association with epilepsy.

AETIOLOGY

The incidence is about 1 in 15,000 births. The metabolic disturbance consists of a failure of the oxidation of phenylalanine to tyrosine. This causes accumulation of phenylalanine in the body and its excretion in the urine. Affected individuals have been treated by the use of a diet low in phenylalanine content.

3. Cretinism

MANIFESTATIONS

(a) Lethargy and slowness,
(b) characteristic cry,
(c) puffiness of face, hands and neck,
(d) subnormal body temperature.

TREATMENT

Thyroid $\frac{1}{2}$ gr per day up to a maximum of 5 gr daily.

4. Turner's Syndrome

MANIFESTATIONS

(a) Subnormality,
(b) ovarian dysgenesis,

(c) dwarfism,
(d) webbing of the neck,
(e) coarctation of aorta.

AETIOLOGY
45 chromosomes.
XO chromosomal constitution.

5. Kleinfelter's Syndrome
MANIFESTATIONS
(a) Subnormality (usually slight),
(b) small testes and aspermia,
(c) gynecomastia.

AETIOLOGY
47 chromosomes.
XXY chromosomal constitution.

6. Hartnup disease
MANIFESTATIONS
(a) Renal aminoaciduria,
(b) pellagrinous skin rashes,
(c) cerebellar ataxia,
(d) subnormality.

AETIOLOGY
(a) Single recessive genetic inheritance,
(b) defect of renal tubular reabsorption,
(c) block in tryptophan metabolism.

7. Maple Sugar disease
MANIFESTATIONS
(a) Urine smelling of maple sugar contains amino acids,
(b) subnormality.

AETIOLOGY

(a) Disordered metabolism of branched chail aliphatic amino acids,
(b) single recessive genetic inheritance.

8. Laurence Moon Biedl Syndrome

MANIFESTATIONS

(a) Obesity,
(b) hypogonadism,
(c) diabetes insipidus,
(d) polydactyly,
(e) pigmented retinitis.

AETIOLOGY

(a) Hypopituitarism, possibly of genetic origin.

GENERAL COMMENTS ON SUBNORMALITY

It is clear that the investigation and treatment of subnormal patients is an area of specialized medical and psychiatric knowledge. For too long subnormality has occupied a lowly place in medical priorities. Custodialism and a pessimistic outlook have now given way to an atmosphere of optimistic enquiry nourished by research.

REFERENCES

BURT C. (1957) Inheritance of Mental Ability. *Nature*, **179**, 1325.

CENTERWALL W. R. *et al.* (1961) Phenyl Ketonuria 1. Dietary Management in Infants and Young Children. 2. Results of Treatment. *J. Pediat.* 59, 93, 102.

JERVIS G. A. (1954) Phenyl Pyruvic Oligophrenia. (Phenylke-tonuria) In Metabolic Diseases of the Nervous System. *Ass. Res. Ment. & Nerv. Dis.* **33,** 259.

LEWIS E. O. (1933) Types of Mental Deficiency and their Social Significance. *J. Ment. Sci.* **79,** 298.

PENROSE L. S. (1961) Mongolism. *Brit. Med. Bull.* **17,** 184.

TIZARD J., GRAD. J. C. (1961) *The Mentally Handicapped and their families.* Maudsley Monograph 7. Oxford University Press.

CHAPTER 9. PSYCHIATRIC DISORDERS IN THE ELDERLY

Normal Ageing

If youth and adolescence are times of emotional development, maturation and turbulence, so old age, is, psychologically speaking, a time of relative stability. However, this relative stability is often more apparent than real and it should be realized that old age often brings psychological difficulties. Quite apart from this the elderly person faces special physical and social problems.

Once an individual becomes old the physical aspects and hazards of ageing become apparent. His joints and skin lose their elasticity and he becomes prone to those common disorders of the heart and circulation which are such an important feature of the morbidity of the sixty to seventy age group. It is unfortunate that at this time in his life the average person usually undergoes a major social change e.g. retirement or widowhood. There are, therefore, obvious sources of stress in old age which merit enumeration.

(a) Increasing physical ill health, e.g. Hypertension, ichaemic heart disease, chronic bronchitis.

(b) Poverty.

(c) Loneliness.

(d) Loss of a marital partner.

(e) Altered social role in a competitive society.

(f) Fear of death.

(g) Malnutrition.

The particular psychological disadvantage of the old person is a lack of flexibility.

In old age personality traits are already well established and patterns of behaviour relatively fixed. It is a commonplace finding that rigidity of outlook and feeling are part of the normal manifestations of ageing.

It is, therefore, always important to bear this in mind when trying to assess the mental state of a supposedly abnormal elderly patient. A certain stubbornness and obstinacy which may be normal in the elderly person may be given undue value by a prejudiced or inexperienced observer.

PSYCHIATRIC SYNDROMES IN OLD AGE

From what has been stated above it will be clear that the special features of psychiatric syndromes in the elderly are related to the fact that the individual's personality is fixed, his capacity for change limited and hence, often, his reaction to a situation more calamitous than if he were twenty years younger.

AFFECTIVE DISORDERS

Are the most important groups of illnesses to consider because the depressive states are so amenable to treatment.

It is, therefore, doubly important that the depressed elderly patient is not overlooked.

It is easy to mistake a state of chronic apathetic depression and suppose that an individual is a lonely old person when in fact he is a lonely depressed old person.

Classically the depressive illness of old age has been described as *involutional melancholia* but there is some controversy as to whether this is an illness peculiar to old age or merely the coincidence of the one with the other.

At all events the syndrome is notable for:

(a) Profound depressive affect.

(b) Striking degrees of agitation.

H

(c) Massive ideas of guilt and self-recrimination, often of delusional intensity.

This variety of affective disorder is not difficult to diagnose. However, lesser degrees of depression may be.

One should, therefore, always be on the lookout for the apathy, hypochondriasis, inertia and sleep disturbance associated with depression.

Hypomanic excitement

In the elderly is not uncommon but is apt to be persistent and again may go unrecognized if not severe. e.g. An 86-year-old man Mr S. was said to be presenting a difficult problem in management in a geriatric ward because of his interfering, restless behaviour. He was described as 'thieving and mischievous'. In fact on examination he presented a typical picture of mild hypomanic excitement with elation and some grandiose ideas. All this settled with appropriate medication.

Treatment

Antidepressive medication is the treatment of choice though severely depressed old people will respond very well to E.C.T. providing their physical conditions permit it.

Imipramine and Amitryptiline are the most frequently used antidepressants in the elderly. Caution should be exercised in commencing these medications since the usual initial dose of 25 mg t.d.s. may induce states of excitement, or in the case of Amitryptiline, excessive drowsiness. It is therefore advisable to start off with 10 mg t.d.s.

PARANOID PSYCHOSES

Acute paranoid reactions are commonly encountered in the elderly. The patient may develop an acute illness in which agitation and persecutory notions are prominent. In many instances a strong *affective colouring* is found, whilst in others there may be evidence of *organic impairment*. Whatever the aetiology it is important to recognize that these acute disturbances, if handled carefully and sensibly, will have a good outcome.

The reaction may have been triggered off by some obvious event in the patient's life such as removal from home to an old people's home, or admission to hospital.

Such a change of environment may be too much for the old person who then becomes frightened, suspicious and bewildered, and if treated tactlessly, even by well-meaning individuals, may 'blow up' into a state of psychotic excitement.

Aetiology
Many paranoid syndromes in the elderly arise as an acute reaction set against a background of organic cerebral impairment. This is most commonly associated with either *cerebral arteriosclerosis* or *senile dementia*. Others are heavily coloured by affective symptoms and are probably *affective in origin*. They respond well to antidepressive treatment.

It should be remembered too that the old person *handicapped by deafness or blindness* is a likely candidate for a paranoid state.

Schizophrenic psychoses can arise in the elderly—these are little different in form from other schizophrenias. Finally the paranoid syndrome may be grafted on to a *lifelong paranoid personality disorder*.

ORGANIC SYNDROMES

Organic syndromes including subacute delirious states superimposed on dementia are commonplace in the elderly. It is not uncommon for such patients to require admission to hospital in an acutely disturbed state in which disorientation and restlessness are manifest.

Aetiology

A typical clinical picture is one of acute confusion with perplexity, restlessness, incoherence of thought and feeling. The most common setting for this is either *cerebral arteriosclerosis* or *senile dementia* but in addition to this *acute confusional episodes in the elderly* can be caused by such events as myocardial infaction, bronchopneumonia, anaemia and uraemia. These four conditions should always be borne in mind. They are easily excluded and investigations aimed at this should be routine in the examination of the confused elderly person.

General Considerations

Any elderly person who develops a psychiatric syndrome should be carefully evaluated in his or her home situation before the decision is taken to admit to a psychiatric hospital. Admission to hospital should only be arranged if there is a clear indication, i.e. if the patient can best be treated in hospital. It is vital that the elderly patient should not lose his or her place in the community. Whitehead has demonstrated convincingly the value of psychiatric admissions on a 'month in and month out' basis even with quite severely demented patients. In addition to this the elderly patient with psychiatric disturbance can be perfectly adequately maintained at day hospitals, or day centres.

The patient's physical health should be carefully investigated and disorders such as chronic bronchitis, ischaemic heart disease, prostatic enlargement, arthritis etc. all searched for and given adequate treatment.

Of course, there are some patients who will require long-term care in mental hospital, e.g. those with severe states of dementia but these should be in the minority. Local Authorities provide residential accommodation for patients with psycho-geriatric disturbance and these services should be utilized wherever possible.

Although in many instances the goals of psychiatric treatment in the elderly patient may be limited, the results are none the less often extremely gratifying. The dramatic relief of the depression previously unrecognized can cause such a radical alteration in the patient's way of life. Simple psychotherapy too is of great value. It is easy to avoid old people and all too often they are ignored and retreat into mildly hostile apathy. Simple discussion of their problems, acknowledgement of their status and awareness of their plight with sympathetic understanding can always produce considerable symptomatic relief.

REFERENCES

ALLISON R. S. (1962) *The Senile Brain: A clinical study.* Edward Arnold, London.

LEWIS A. (1955) Mental Aspects of Ageing. *Ciba Foundation Coll. Ageing* 1, 32. Churchill. London.

POST F. (1962) The Significance of Affective Symptoms in Old Age. *Maudsley Monographs 10.*

WHITEHEAD J. A. (1965) A Comprehensive Psycho-Geriatric Service. *Lancet*, ii, 583–6.

CHAPTER 10. PSYCHIATRY AND THE LAW

THE MENTAL HEALTH ACT, 1959

Historical Background

The history of the care of the mentally ill is on the whole a grim story consisting mainly of neglect, indifference and ill treatment, despite islands of progress. From time to time reforming persons halted this process and laws were passed to regulate the running of asylums for the insane and protect the inmates.

The main purpose of such institutions was custodial—if a patient entered, he stood only a small chance of returning to the world since little active treatment could be offered and society did not welcome his return, believing him to be dangerous and beyond hope of improvement.

The nineteenth century saw emphasis on *the moral treatment of the insane* i.e. treating patients like human beings, and a great deal was accomplished to improve the care of patients, finding them useful occupations, removing restraint and encouraging a more hopeful attitude.

Nevertheless legislation was cumbersome, and even as late as 1890 the passage of the Lunacy Acts did not make the position easier. If anything the mental hospitals were fixed in a custodial role, since voluntary admission to mental hospital was impossible. A step forward occurred in 1930, with the Mental Treatment Act, which enabled people to enter hospital voluntarily. In the past twenty years, as knowledge and therapeutic zeal increased, it became apparent that a less unwieldy set of laws was needed. This culminated in 1959 with the *Mental Health Act.*

The Act itself

This is a comprehensive act which repeals the Lunacy Acts of 1890 and the Mental Treatment Act of 1930. The most important general features are as follows:

1. Control of mental hospitals and mental nursing homes etc., passes from the *Board of Control* to the *National Health Service.*

2. Informal admission of patients is encouraged.

3. The procedure surrounding compulsory admission to hospital is made more clinical and less formal and intimidating.

4. The role of the local authority in mental health services is defined.

The act is divided into nine parts.

Part 1 repeals previous legislation, defines and classifies mental disorder and proclaims informal admission (Sec. 1–5)
Part 2 deals with the role of the local authority (Sec. 6–13)
Part 3 deals with nursing homes etc. (Sec. 14–24)
Part 4 deals with compulsory admission to hospital (Sec. 25–59)
Part 5 deals with criminal patients (Sec. 60–80)
Part 6 deals with transfer of patients (Sec. 81–96)
Part 7 deals with special hospitals (for dangerous and violent patients) (Sec. 97–99)
Part 8 deals with management of property and affairs of patients (Sec. 100–121)
Part 9 Miscellaneous (Sec. 122–154)

The sections of the Act of most interest to students are sections 25, 26, 29 and 30.

SECTION 25

Under this section of the Act it is possible to detain a patient in a mental hospital for a period not exceeding 28 days, for the purpose of observation. A medical recommendation to this effect is signed by two doctors—

(1) the patient's own doctor (where possible),

(2) a doctor recognized by the Act as having special experience in psychiatry.

The application for admission is made by the nearest relative, or if not available a mental Welfare Officer.

SECTION 26

Is the section under which an order for *treatment* is made, on the grounds that the patient is a danger to himself or others or is not suitable for informal admission. This is valid for 1 yr. The patient has the right of appeal against this after 6 months to a review tribunal.

SECTION 29

Provides a means of *emergency admission*. It permits the patient to be detained for 72 h pending conversion to either S.25 or informal status.

The application is made by the nearest relative or Mental Welfare Officer, and the medical recommendation is made by any registered practitioner providing he has seen the patient within 24 h of signing.

SECTION 30

Provides for retention in hospital of a patient already in, who becomes ill and requires compulsory observation. This order, signed by the doctor in charge of the patient, authorizes his being kept in hospital for 3 days pending further action.

Criminal Responsibility

It is an established principle of English Law that a man is responsible for his own actions—that is to say that he intends their result. Therefore it follows that in the eyes of the law he must bear the responsibility for them. In the case of serious offences, responsibility is the more likely to be questioned. In the case of an individual suffering from mental illness committing a crime, it has been for many years argued that the man's state of mind must impair his responsibility for his acts. This has, however, not been easy to establish in a court of law since the law assumes everyone is sane, and insanity has to be proven. Since 1843 the courts have used the MacNaughten Rules as a test of insanity. These rules arose following the trial for murder of Daniel MacNaughten who killed Sir Robert Peel's private secretary. MacNaughten had paranoid delusions and was acquitted on the direction of the judge.

Subsequently judges formulated the rules as they have been known ever since, as a series of answers to questions put to them by the House of Lords. In practice the rules seek the answers to the questions:

(1) Regarding the offence, did the accused know the nature and quality of the act?

(2) If he did, did he know he was doing wrong?

(3) If he knew the nature and quality of the act, was he labouring under a delusion?

Despite their apparent simplicity, the rules can be difficult to apply and make for only a limited acknowledgement of impaired responsibility. For years they have been the subject of controversy, both here and in the United States. Nevertheless they are still widely applied as tests of insanity in capital cases.

Since the Homicide Act of 1957 the Law in England and Wales has acknowledged the concept of diminished responsibility, which can be invoked if an accused person is shown to be suffering from 'such abnormality of mind . . . as substantially to impair his responsibility'. The concept of diminished responsibility has not been accepted without reserve, and it has been pointed out that once allowance is made for diminished responsibility one is calling into question the whole idea of criminal responsibility at any level.

Testamentary Capacity
The ability to make a valid will depends on the possession of a 'sound disposing mind'. This is not defined in law but the con-

cept is derived from the notion that the person concerned should fulfil the following criteria: he should understand the implications of the act of making a will, have a good idea of the extent of the estate and know who are the likely beneficiaries. Mental illness, whether through psychosis or organic cerebral disease, does not automatically debar someone from making a valid will, since even in chronic schizophrenia and in dementia there are often well-preserved areas of lucidity and contact with reality. A doctor should never witness a will irrespective of whether or no he is a beneficiary.

REFERENCES

GLUECK S. (1963) *Psychiatry and the Law*. Tavistock, London.
SLATER E. (1954) The MacNaughten Rules and Modern Concepts of Responsibility. *Brit. med. J.* ii, 713.

CHAPTER 11. TREATMENT
IN PSYCHIATRY

The term 'Treatment' is used in a wide sense in psychiatry; specific remedies for illnesses of known aetiology are practically unknown, so treatment tends to be empirical and eclectic. Treatment therefore includes any measures used:

    (a) to influence the patient's mental state, and

    (b) to assist in his rehabilitation and return to the community.

The measures used comprise the following groups:

(a) psychological	psychotherapy behaviour therapy	used to deal with individual's symptoms, illness and personality
(b) physical	pharmacologic agents e.g. sedatives tranquillizers antidepressive drugs	used in acute psychoses, depressive illness and 'maintenance' treatment of chronic illness
(c) occupational	occupational therapy	used to divert, stimulate, entertain and encourage the patient's activity and interest
	industrial therapy	plays an important part in rehabilitation by giving the patient the chance to work and earn in a sheltered environment

Certain measures may be of most value in the acute illness, e.g. physical treatment; others may be of most value in rehabilitation, e.g. industrial therapy. Patients should receive help in as many ways as possible. The acute illness may be controlled by tranquillizers which restore the patient's contact with reality and enable him to participate more successfully in psychotherapy, and derive some benefit from a therapeutic environment. Providing the environment is permissive and friendly, it is therapeutic rather than antitherapeutic. Social forces too, are important in colouring illness and adding features which are neither symptoms or signs of illness but merely behaviour patterns imposed by the environment. Violent behaviour has become less common since this was realized. The struggling patient brought into hospital and hurled into a padded room, isolated in total darkness, would be less than normal if he did not react in hostile fashion towards his surroundings.

It is important to realize that any hospital admission provokes anxiety mainly because of the uncertainty that the patient experiences and also because he feels his individuality threatened right from the beginning by simple things like having to undress and get into bed. After this, much that goes on in hospital seems to reinforce the feeling of isolation and lack of identity so that if the atmosphere is worsened by heightened uncertainty, tension and suppressed violence—all of which can be commonplace in a badly run psychiatric ward —one soon has all the ingredients for a situation of the sort which Kafka has described in such frightening fashion.

Future planning of district psychiatric services in England and Wales should help considerably towards finally removing the stigma and general unease that surround mental hospital admission. The psychiatric unit in a general hospital, working in close cooperation with local services, should provide the best way to use hospital admission without damaging the patient.

PSYCHOLOGICAL TREATMENT

1. Individual Psychotherapy
Psychotherapy is treatment based on verbal communication

between patient and doctor and the formation of a therapeutic relationship between them.

The simplest form, and the most widely practised is *supportive psychotherapy*, in which the patient is encouraged to talk freely about himself and his symptoms and problems without exploring his unconscious mental life. No attempt is made to give the patient insight about the possible origins of his difficulties. His defences are shored up rather than broken down.

Psychoanalysis is the most important type of analytic psychotherapy. The term 'psychoanalysis' is used in two main ways, first it refers to a form of psychotherapy, and secondly it gives the name to the school of psychology founded by S. Freud.

Psychoanalytic theory is a theory of personality structure and development which stresses the fundamental importance of childhood experience in forming the personality. Freud based his theory on observations made on patients he had treated. Classical Freudian theory has been modified by his followers but the central hypothesis is that human behaviour is determined predominantly by unconscious forces and motives springing from primitive emotional needs.

In psychoanalysis the analyst seeks to explore and modify the personality structure of the patient by intensive and prolonged exploration of this unconscious mental life. This is achieved by use of the technique of *free association*. The patient lies on a couch and allows his thoughts to wander in any direction—in this way dredging up unconscious material of which he has previously apparently been quite unaware. The reason for getting the patient to lie down is so as to cut down to a minimum visual stimuli which might distract. The analyst interprets to the patient the symbolic meaning of his dreams and fantasies helping him towards insight about himself. It is necessarily a prolonged and time consuming process.

Analytic psychotherapy short of full-scale psychoanalysis, is commoner and less cumbersome a process, and tends to be concerned with more clearly defined goals such as:

(a) resolution of conflict,

(b) working through problems and viewing them in a different light,

(c) the relief of pent-up feelings.

The relationship between doctor and patient in psychotherapy is of paramount importance. Much of the content of interviews is so to speak 'hot material' and the patient soon invests the therapist with a good deal of feeling. Feelings of dependence, love, affection and hostility are common and the therapist has to know how to handle them and how to interpret their meaning to the patient. A personal analysis provides the only training for the psychoanalyst.

A non-analytic psychotherapist gains a great deal from a personal analysis but if this is not possible the good psychotherapist needs to be intelligent, intuitive, patient and above all, flexible.

Individual psychotherapy does not end with psychoanalysis. In fact psychoanalysis is probably the least commonly practised form of psychotherapy since it is time consuming and uneconomical. On the other hand most psychotherapies owe a good deal to psychoanalytic theory without acknowledging it. In recent years there has been a move away from the 'classical' psychoanalytic type therapy towards briefer psychotherapies. Some concentrate on the meaning of the symptom, i.e. 'what sort of help is this patient *really* asking for?' Others pay particular attention to the 'here and now' situation, moving the patient all the time towards solving a particular problem in his life that he appears say to be avoiding. While other psychotherapies are directed at the patient in a way that does not seem explicit but which moves the patient towards independence and self-reliance. Other psychotherapies are existential not only in following existential philosophy but also in practical terms in that they encourage the patient towards responsibility for the self and one's actions, at the same time helping the patient to look at himself as a person in the world and to achieve some understanding of the meaning and significance of his existence.

2. Group Psychotherapy

In group therapy the main focus of interest is on the inter-relationships within the group, rather than on the highly personal relationships as in individual therapy. Problems are shared in the group situation, and patients are able to see their own difficulties in interpersonal relationships reflected in the group, and so in a different light. Also they are subject to criticism, encouragement and support from other members of the group.

In practice groups should be small—about twelve members being the ideal number. It is found useful to select members of similar ages and with equal division of sexes. The therapist sits with the group—topics are discussed freely, the therapist adopts a non-directive role, avoiding domination or direction of the group but preventing them from straying into defensive irrelevancies.

3. Abreaction

Is the name given to a therapeutic process in which a patient relives an important past experience which has contributed significantly to the development of his illness. The re-enactment is accompanied by discharge of pent-up feeling. Freud found this happening to his patients, particularly under hypnosis, and he reasoned that it would be valuable to induce such states so that the patient would benefit by the emotional discharge. The technique of abreaction is used mainly in acute conversion hysteria precipitated by traumatic events, e.g. war-time disasters. Various methods other than hypnosis have been used to bring about a state of altered consciousness conducive to abreaction. The most widely used is the slow intravenous injection of a 5 per cent solution of sodium amytal.

4. Behaviour Therapy

Is the general name given to a relatively recent form of psychological treatment. Behaviour therapy has its roots in behaviouristic psychology as opposed to psychotherapy which is founded on dynamic psychology.

Behaviouristic psychology explains human behaviour in terms of stimulus—response mechanisms. Behaviour is regarded as learnt by Pavlovian conditioning processes governed by such processes or drive reduction. Thus neurotic behaviour is simply explained in terms of maladaptive behaviour rather than being linked with complicated intra personal, emotional development.

It follows from this view of neurotic illness that if the neurotic symptom is removed, the illness disappears too—an entirely opposite view to the psychodynamic one which sees symptoms as symbolic representations of internal conflict. A behaviouristic explanation of a phobic anxiety state would be that the patient has become conditioned to experience anxiety whenever he perceives certain signals and that this conditioned response has gradually generalized so that it is triggered off by a wide variety of signals.

Behaviour therapy seeks to eradicate the maladaptive response by a process of desensitization. Wolpe has pointed out that the anxiety response can be inhibited by placing the individual in situations resembling those which provoke anxiety but which are sufficiently unlike them not to trigger off any anxiety. This builds up a generalizing process of reciprocal inhibition of anxiety, which is reinforced by rewards in the form of further anxiety-free situations.

PHYSICAL TREATMENT

Nowhere is empiricism more evident than in the sphere of physical treatment in psychiatry. Methods have appeared; a remarkable array of drugs is on the market; all are greeted with initial uncritical enthusiasm and later more soberly evaluated. The whole question of the use of physical treatments has aroused strong feelings on both sides. Nevertheless it is a fact that certain physical treatments have established themselves as important therapies which have revolutionized psychiatry.

1. Psychotropic Drugs

Psychotropic drugs are special in that they alter feeling, perception and behaviour without significantly altering consciousness. The study of such drugs, i.e. Psychopharmacology, has not only produced a large range of drugs used in treatment but has also suggested possible lines of research in the biochemistry of mental illness. The *Cerebral Amine* theory of depression is a good example. According to this theory the central transmitting amines are linked to depression in that it appears that depression can be associated with a low concentration of amines and mania with excessive concentrations. The amines concerned are Noradrenaline, 5-Hydroxy tryptamine (5-HTT or serotonin) and dopamine. The tricyclic antidepressants are thought to act by blocking the reabsorption of free amines and the monoamine oxidase inhibitors to act by preventing de-oxidative deamination, i.e. in either case causing higher amine concentrations.

The important psychotropic drugs include:
Neuroleptics (Major tranquillizers)
Antidepressants
Tranquillizers (Anxiolytic drugs)
Lithium

2. Neuroleptics and Tranquillizers

Tranquillizers are drugs which alter behaviour without impairing consciousness. Their place in psychiatry dates from 1953 when the tranquillizing effects of *Chlorpromazine* were first demonstrated. *Chlorpromazine* was the first of the phenothiazines to come into use, and the majority of the tranquillizers

I

in present use belong to the phenothiazine series. Phenothiazines all have the basic structure:

where R1 and/or R2 are side chains varying from one phenothiazine to another.

Chlorpromazine (Largactil) is most useful in calming psychotic excitement whether organic, affective or schizophrenic in origin. It is widely used in the maintenance treatment of chronic psychotic patients but the usefulness here is much less certain. It can be administered by either the intramuscular or oral route. *Dosage* is up to a maximum of 600 mg per day in divided doses, though a maximum of 400 mg per day is rarely exceeded.

The most serious *side effects* include anaemia, agranulocytosis and jaundice. Less important effects include hypotensive attacks, photosensitivity and dermatitis.

Chlorpromazine potentiates the action of barbiturates, alcohol, anaesthetics and narcotic drugs.

Promazine (Sparine) is a phenothiazine of similar structure and action though probably less powerful weight for weight than chlorpromazine. Side effects such as rashes and hypotension may be less than with chlorpromazine.

Thioridazine (Melleril) has a similar dosage range to chlorpromazine, and similar actions.

Trifluoperazine (Stelazine) is an important drug of the prochlorperazine series (derived from the penothiazines). It is said to have an alerting and antihallucinogenic effect in contrast to the sedative effect of the other phenothiazines. It is widely used in the treatment of both acute and chronic schizophrenic patients. It can be administered parenterally or orally. *Dosage* ranges from 5–40 mg per day in divided doses. There is evidence to suggest that in small doses (2 mg t.d.s.) it is useful in the treatment of chronic anxiety states.

Fluphenazine enanthate (Moditen). This is a long-acting phenothiazine drug which when injected intramuscularly acts for between 2 and 3 weeks. Has the advantage of being very useful for the patient who is uncooperative about taking medication. The incidence of extrapyramidal side effects is high but this is usually avoided by giving the patient routine anti-parkinsonian medication. The usual practice is to give a test dose of 12·5 mg followed by a once fortnightly dose of 25 mg of the Moditen.

Fluphenazine decanoate (Modecate) has replaced fluphenazine enanthate since it need only be given once monthly.

Side effects
The most common are neurological syndromes affecting the extra-pyramidal pathways:
  (1) motor restlessness (akathisia)
  (2) facial rigidity ⎫
  (3) stiffness of limbs ⎭   Parkinsonian syndrome
  (4) persistent tongue protrusion
  (5) dystonic movements of the head and neck.
These neurological side effects can be well controlled by use of antiparkinsonian drugs such as Orphenadrine (Disipal) etc.

3. Antidepressant Drugs
Drugs used in the treatment of depression fall into two main groups:
(a) The Tricyclic series
(b) The monoamine oxidase inhibitors.

The first drugs used in the treatment of depression were *amphetamine and its derivatives*. They had the advantage of cheapness and a lack of minor side effects. Unfortunately the dangers of abuse and addiction have made their use undesirable. Also they are not effective in severe depression.

(a) THE TRICYCLIC SERIES

The most important drugs of this series are: Imipramine (Tofranil); Amitryptiline (Triptizol); Nortryptiline (Aventyl).

Imipramine is chemically similar to Chlorpromazine being an imino dibenzyl derivative and has been used in the treatment of depression since 1959.

Dosage range 25–75 mg t.d.s.

Side effects include dryness of the mouth, blurring of vision, wakefulness, constipation, states of excitement and hypotensive attacks.

Amitryptiline is given in a dosage range of 25–75 mg t.d.s. Side effects include dryness of the mouth, drowsiness, blurred vision, constipation and states of excitement.

Nortryptiline is given in a dosage range of 25 mg t.d.s. to 50 mg t.d.s. It is said to be more quick in action than imipramine or amitryptiline.

Anafranil, dosage range 25 mg to 50 mg t.d.s.—is a recently introduced tricyclic antidepressant which is reported as being quicker in action than others.

Lentizol. This is a sustained release preparation of amitryptiline given in 25 mg or 50 mg capsules. The advantage is this is useful for the patient who forgets to take tablets during the day and thus can manage on one capsule at night.

Other tricyclic antidepressants include Protryptiline (Concordin) (up to 45 mg daily), Iprindole (Prondol) (up to 90 mg daily) and Trimipramine (Surmontil) (up to 100 mg daily). In fact, the tricyclic antidepressants can be given in one daily dose; this makes their administration a good deal easier.

(b) THE MONOAMINE OXIDASE INHIBITORS

The first demonstration of the euphoriant effect of this group of drugs was that INAH used in the treatment of tuberculosis made patients euphoric. Since then a large number of MAO inhibitors have been developed. Probably the most common in use are: Isocarboxazid (Marplan) Dosage range 10–30 mg t.d.s.; Phenelzine (Nardil) Dosage range 15–30 mg t.d.s.;

Tranylcypromine (Parnate) Dosage range 15 mg t.d.s. to 15 mg q.d.s.

Side effects

(1) Potentiation of barbiturates, alcohol, tranquillizers, opiates and Pethidine. For this reason their use presents special hazards in anaesthesia.

(2) States of excitement and agitation

(3) Hypotension

(4) Hypertensive crises. These occur in certain patients if they eat foods containing *tyramine* such as certain cheeses, yeast extracts and broad bean pods. Patients should be warned not to eat these foods. The crises when they occur are characterized by severe headache which can simulate subarachnoid haemorrhage.

(5) Liver damage. This has been found most commonly in the Hydrazine series (phenelzine, isocarboxazid).

(6) Other common side effects include oedema, sexual impotence and failure of orgasm; also dryness of the mouth, blurred vision and constipation.

Combinations of MAO inhibitors and Tricyclic antidepressants can be dangerous and are probably best avoided or left to the expert.

GENERAL OBSERVATIONS ON THE USE OF
ANTIDEPRESSIVE DRUGS

Though they are widely prescribed, there is by no means universal agreement either as to their efficacy or mode of action. Controlled trials have revealed conflicting results. On the one hand there are those workers who are convinced that antidepressive drugs exert a specific effect on the supposed depressive process, whilst on the other there are those who claim that the drugs act merely by their sedative effect on agitation and anxiety. It has been pointed out that depression has a high rate of natural remission and that the enthusiasm for the effects of antidepressive drugs may be accounted for by this alone. Whatever the facts may turn out to be, one thing seems certain and that is that physicians have become more alerted to depression and its existence as a condition meriting attention and treatment.

4. Drugs used in the treatment of anxiety

Apart from short acting barbiturates which are widely used, there are two tranquillizers in common use. They are:

Chloriazepoxide (Librium) 10–40 mg t.d.s.
Diazepam (Valium) 10–40 mg t.d.s.

5. Vitamins

Large doses of vitamins of the B group are used routinely:

(a) in the treatment of delirium tremens,
(b) in the treatment of subacute delirious states.

6. Insulin is used:

(a) as an appetizer,
(b) in modified Insulin Treatment. This is a form of treatment used in states of anxiety. The patient is given increasing doses of soluble insulin in the morning with the object of producing a drowsy relaxed state and inducing hunger. The treatment is terminated by a large carbohydrate meal.

7. Electro-convulsive Therapy

Of all physical treatments E.C.T. is apparently the most successful, yet its mode of action is unknown and in some quarters its use is viewed with suspicion. Speculative theories of a neurophysiologic sort suggest that the convulsion alters the conditionability of an intricate system or that in some way it alters the level of arousal of the central nervous system. Other theorists suggest that in some unknown way it alters the balance of a central mood regulating mechanism. These tend to represent the views of those favouring its use.

Those who are on the whole opposed to its use tend to suggest that it is a form of 'shock' treatment which in a way 'shocks' the patient into altered behaviour as in the past patients were 'shocked' by sudden immersion or being whirled around in revolving chairs. It has also been suggested that it is the sudden loss of consciousness which affects the patient. Nevertheless there is more uniformity of agreement about its usefulness than is the case with drugs.

ORIGINS

It was first used in 1938 by Cerletti and Bini. It had previously been incorrectly supposed that there was a negative correlation between epilepsy and schizophrenia and on the basis of this it was suggested that schizophrenia might be treated by convulsions. Meduna started by using chemically induced convulsions in 1935, while Cerletti and Bini were the first to use electrically induced fits.

The results in treating depression were soon shown to be successful. Depressive mood and agitation were replaced by normal mood within days of starting treatment, and it is in the treatment of depression that E.C.T. has an established place. It is successful in approximately 85 per cent of cases of depression. Whether or not it prevents recurrences is questionable but it does shorten the illness.

Its place in the treatment of schizophrenia is controversial, though most experienced workers suggest that it should always be tried. Acute schizophrenic episodes and schizo-affective illnesses respond best to it.

TECHNIQUE

A typical machine gives a 100 v discharge for one sec. This induces instant loss of consciousness followed by convulsion. Nowadays it is usual to give modified E.C.T. and the practice is to modify it by using intravenous anaesthesia (Thiopentone 200–250 mg in a 5 per cent solution) with a muscle relaxant (Scoline or Brevidil) to prevent injury by violent muscular contractions. Oxygen is used to ventilate the patient, and the convulsion is induced. Recovery of consciousness is rapid e.g. within 10 min, and discomfort is no more than a pin prick in the arm. Atropine 1/75 gr is given intravenously with the Thiopentone.

Treatment is given twice weekly and the patient assessed between treatments. A course of treatment is not prescribed; it is preferable to stop when the patient is better. One should rarely give more than twelve treatments.

HAZARDS OF E.C.T.

These are:

Major

1. Normal anaesthetic hazards.
2. Special cardiovascular hazard, e.g. induction of cardiac arrhythmia.
3. Injury to tongue,
    teeth
    bones—longbones
    —scapula
    —crush fractures of vertebral bodies.

Minor

4. amenorrhea
5. headache
6. burns
7. memory loss
8. confusional states.

8. Leucotomy

The various types of leucotomy operation are all aimed at the relief of persistent tension. This is achieved by dividing connections between the frontal lobes and the Thalamus. The operation probably shows the best results when the tension arises in depressive states but it has also been used in obsessional disorder and in chronic schizophrenia.

The operation is now less widely performed since the advent of the tranquillizers and since its dangers have been more fully appreciated, nevertheless in carefully selected cases it continues to be used in the relief of chronic tension states.

OCCUPATIONAL

1. Occupational Therapy

For many years it has been realized that work can be a source of diversion to the disturbed patient. Nowadays the Occupational Therapist has a wide range of activities to offer the psychiatric patient. These include art and craft work which can calm the anxious patient or revive the interest of the retarded depressive. Tasks can be provided for the brain damaged patient which may afford him some degree of satisfaction.

Also the Occupational Therapist can assess the limits of such a patient's ability and help to provide him with a suitable environment. In rehabilitation the O.T. Department can help to plan a patient's daily round of activity to prepare for the return home by helping him to acquire new skills or refurbish old ones. The housewife can be particularly helped in this direction by the provision of a kitchen unit in the O.T. Department. Ideally Occupational Therapy should be realistic and diverse and as far removed as possible from the traditional picture of basket making or the manufacture of useless ornaments.

2. Industrial Therapy

This is an attempt to provide the patient with a working day, a regular wage and the prospects of working outside hospital.

It provides a sheltered working environment for the chronic patient where he can learn, practise and gain confidence in new skills.

In many hospitals light assembly work etc. is done on a contract basis with local firms and after a patient has 'proved himself', he can then go out to work.

Rehabilitation of chronic patients, particularly chronic schizophrenics, is a difficult task. Patients need graded tasks, much encouragement, careful assessment and supervision. In this the doctor is aided by many people including:

(1) nurses with special training and experience,
(2) social workers,
(3) psychologists,
(4) disablement resettlement officers.

SOCIAL MEASURES

The Psychiatric Social Worker

The P.S.W. occupies a central place in psychiatric practice bringing to it not only a knowledge of social factors and their importance in the aetiology of illness but also more sophisticated awareness of psychodynamics than that possessed by the non-psychiatric social worker. This is not to suggest that P.S.W. should be some form of psychotherapist manqué since this would mean too limited a function. The work of the P.S.W. includes such diverse activities as:

(1) collection of data,
(2) highlighting of areas of social relevance in a patient's life situation,
(3) direct counselling about concrete social problems such as finance, housing, etc.,
(4) social casework: this is a therapeutic technique in which the P.S.W. helps the patient to handle his problems, and relate them to his social situation,
(5) helping a patient to get psychiatric advice,
(6) prophylaxis of psychiatric disorder,
(7) group discussions with the spouses of patients who have a common problem (e.g. alcoholics' wives),
(8) after care and follow up.

The Therapeutic Community

All hospitals are frightening places for the majority of patients, and mental hospitals are particularly so, since often they tend to be large, gaunt buildings with long anonymous corridors. In fact if one were to try and devise a way of making a patient worse one could hardly improve on traditional mental hospital custodial care, which tended to reduce patients to nameless lost creatures, with no identity. In fairness to those who worked in such conditions it should be pointed out that they did not have the advantages of the tranquillizing drugs of today nor enthusiastic support except from a few. It is also incorrect to suppose that 'open door' policies are a twentieth-century phenomenon. They are really an extension of the best of English nineteenth-century psychiatry. Unfortunately, as is often the case, pioneering ideas were forgotten and had to be rediscovered.

The moment anyone enters *any* hospital an attack is made on his existence as an individual—his clothes are removed and he is put to bed and he becomes another patient. In general hospitals this matters less since the duration of stay is short and the experience is soon forgotten. But for the psychiatric patient it can be disastrous, since he may be entering hospital for a long stay. Before the importance of social factors in influencing mental illness was generally appreciated, the object was to make the patient conform to a number of arbitrary behavioural standards often of a fairly absurd sort, as quickly as possible. Authority was hierarchical and not to be defied. This made tension increase and violence the more likely.

Patients soon learnt to survive by adapting themselves into numbed acquiescence with consequent loss of initiative and drive, so called 'institutional neurosis'. This was aided by isolation from visitors and lack of activity.

Belatedly it has been realized that the community in which the patient lives can have either a therapeutic or an anti-therapeutic effect and attempts are now made to produce a hospital environment which preserves the patient's individuality and stimulates him to activity and a return to the world outside.

Emphasis is laid on freeing the lines of communication between medical and nursing staff and encouraging free discussion between patients and staff, thus removing artificial and meaningless barriers. Of course running hospitals in this way means more work and more trouble as opposed to the apparent calm of a traditional 'well run' hospital supervised by a superintendent delegating authority downwards. It means more work, but less misery and more hope. Psychiatric patients need hope, noise, colour and activity. Too often their lives can be spent in a grey silence. Anyone who can prevent this is performing a therapeutic act.

REFERENCES

EYSENCK H. J. (1960) *Behaviour Therapy and the Neuroses*. Pergamon, London.

FINESINGER J. E. (1948) Psychiatric interviewing. *Amer. J. Psychiat.* **105**, 187.

HORDERN A. & HAMILTON M. (1963) Drugs and moral treatment. *Brit. J. Psychiat.* **109**, 500.

MAY A. R. (1961) Prescribing community care for the mentally ill. *Lancet*, **1**, 760.

RAPAPORT R. N. (1960) *Community as Doctor*. Tavistock, London.

REES W. L. (1966) Drugs used in the Treatment of Psychiatric Disorders. *Abstr. Wld. Medicine.* **39**, 129–40.

STANTON A. H. & SCHWARTZ M. S. (1954) The mental hospital. Basic Books, New York.

TOOTH G. C. & BROOK E. M. (1961) Trends in the mental hospital population and their effect on future planning. *Lancet*, **1**, 710

WOLPE J. (1958) *Psychotherapy by Reciprocal Inhibition*. Stanford University Press, California.

INDEX

Abreaction 73, 115
Addiction, see dependence
Addison's disease 31
Admission to hospital, effects of
 112, 126
Adolescent crisis of identity
 18, 19
Affect, incongruity of 45
Affective disorder 17ff
 in the elderly 101, 102
Ageing 100
Alcoholics Anonymous 83
Alcoholic hallucinosis 81
Alcoholism
 acute 79
 chronic 79
 delirium tremens 81
 Korsakov's syndrome 82, 60
 treatment 82
Alzheimer's disease 63
Amitryptiline 120
Analytic psychotherapy 23
Antidepressive drugs 119
Anxiety 6, 17
 aetiology 18
 diagnosis 21
 manifestations 20
 treatment 21

Barbiturates 85
 intoxication 85
 withdrawal fits 85
Behaviour therapy 23, 24, 116
Bleuler 39
Body build
 in affective disorder 27
 in schizophrenia 40

Carbon monoxide poisoning
 dementia following 58
Cardiovascular system
 cerebral effects in heart
 failure 61

Catatonic schizophrenia 47
Catastrophic reaction 56
Cerebral arteriosclerosis 58, 62
Cerebral tumour 64
 frontal 65
 temporal 65
 third ventricle 65
Chromosomal abnormalities
 in Down's syndrome 95
 in Kleinfelter's syndrome 97
 in Turner's syndrome 96
Community Care 50, 51
Compulsive, see obsessional
Constitution
 in anxiety 19
 in affective disorder 27
Cretinism 96
Criminal responsibility 108,
 109

Delirium
 definition 6, 53
 manifestations 53, 54
 tremens 81, 82
Delusion
 definition 7
 in schizophrenia 44
 systems of 47
Delusional ideas 7
Dementia
 definition 6
 in alcoholism 82
 in tumours 58, 64
 in G.P.I. 61
 in Huntington's chorea 63
 presenile 63
 senile 62
Dependence, drug 84
 opiate 84
 etiology 87
 sedative 85
 stimulant 86
 hallucinogenic 86

Depersonalization 6, 7
Depression 25
  reactive 25, 26
  endogenous 26
  aetiology 26ff
  in the elderly 101
  manifestations 29ff
  treatment 33ff
Derealization 7
Disulfiram 83
Down's syndrome 95

Echolalia 48
Echopraxia 48
Elderly patient
  normal ageing 100
  personality traits in 100, 101
  affective disorder in 101
  paranoid psychoses in 102
  organic syndromes 103
  general considerations 104
Electro-convulsive Therapy 122
  in depression 33
  in mania 37
  in schizophrenia 50
  origins of 122
  technique 123
  risks of 124
Epilepsy 63
Examination of patient 5

Family history 4
Flight of ideas 7
Fluphenazine enanthate 119
Fluphenazine decanoate 119
Free association 113
Freud 73, 113

General paresis (G.P.I.) 61
Group psychotherapy 115

Hallucinations
  definition 8
  in organic states 54
  in schizophrenia 46
Hallucinogenic drugs 86
Hartnup disease 97
Head injury 62
Hebephrenia 47

Hereditary factors
  in affective disorder 26
  in schizophrenia 39
  in Huntington's chorea 63
History taking 2, 3
Huntington's chorea 63
Hypomania 34
  in the elderly 102
Hypochondriasis 8
Hysteria
  aetiology 71
  conversion 70
  diagnosis 71, 72
  personality 69
  symptoms 70
  treatment 72, 73

Ideas of reference 8
Illusions 8
Iminodibenzyl derivatives 119
Industrial therapy 125
Insulin 122
Intelligence
  definition 89
  quotient 90
  tests 15, 90, 91
  subnormality 89

Korsakov's syndrome 60, 82

Learning
  and conditioning 20
  relation to anxiety 20
  and behaviour therapy 23, 24
Legal aspects of psychiatry 106ff
Leucotomy 78, 124
Lithium 37

MacNaughten Rules 109
Mania 34
Mannerisms 9
Memory defect 54, 56
Mental Health Act 106, 107, 108
Methadone 85
Mono amine oxidase inhibitors 120
  side effects 121
Myxoedema 31

Neurosis 9
  neuroticism 19

Obsessional disorder 75
  personality 75
  phenomena 9
Occupational therapy 125
Organic syndromes 53ff

Paranoid 9, 10
Paranoid Schizophrenia 48
Paranoid Psychoses in the
  Elderly 102, 103
Passivity feelings 10
Pellagra 60
Personal history 5
Personality 66
  abnormal 66, 67
  hysterical 69
  schizoid 40
  obsessional 75
Phenothiazines 117, 118
Phenyl Pyruvic Oligophrenia 96
Pick's disease 63
Psychiatric interview 1
Psychiatric Social Worker 126
Psychoanalysis 113
Psychopathic Personality 67, 68
Psychosis 9
Psychoses in epilepsy 63, 64
Psychotherapy 22, 112, 113, 114
Psychotropic drugs 117ff

Retardation 29

Schizophrenia 10, 39
  aetiology 39-42
  clinical types 47ff
  community care in 50
  delusions in 44
  manifestations 43
  thought disorder 10, 43
  treatment 49
Sleep disturbance
  in depression 30
Social Class, in Affective disorder 27
Subnormality 89
Stimulant Drugs 86
Suicide in depression 32

Temporal lobe epilepsy 63
Testamentary capacity 109
Therapeutic community 126,
  127
Tranquillizers 117ff
Treatment 111ff
Tricyclic antidepressants 119
Turner's syndrome 96

Vitamin deficiency 60

Wechsler adult intelligence scale
  15
Wernicke's encephalopathy 60